The ultima CHOCOLATE *Cookbook*

Styling DONNA HAY
Photography WILLIAM MEPPEM

A J.B. Fairfax Press Publication

INTRODUCTION

Whatever the occasion, chocolate is a celebration all of its own. This collection of mouth-watering cakes, puddings and desserts is guaranteed to gladden the hearts and delight the taste buds of chocolate lovers everywhere. Luscious cakes and gâteaux, creamy desserts and puddings, fresh fruit combinations, feather-light soufflés and chocolate box treats, all are represented here. Whether you yearn for old favourites, chocolatey home-bakes or a spectacular centrepiece for that special celebration, these recipes are sure to satisfy the longings of even the most discerning chocoholics.

EDITORIAL
Food Editor: Rachel Blackmore
Editors: Kirsten John, Linda Venturoni
Editorial and Production Assistant: Danielle Thiris
Editorial Coordinator: Margaret Kelly
UK Food Consultant: Katie Swallow

Photography: William Meppem
Styling and Food: Donna Hay
Recipe Development: Jody Vassallo
Food Stylist's Assistants: Jo Kennedy, Leisel Rodgers, Darrienne Sutton

DESIGN AND PRODUCTION
Manager: Sheridan Carter
Layout and Design: Lulu Dougherty
Senior Production Editor: Anna Maquire
Production Editor: Sheridan Packer
Cover Design: Michelle Withers

Published by J.B. Fairfax Press Pty Limited
80-82 McLachlan Avenue
Rushcutters Bay, NSW 2011, Australia
A.C.N. 003 738 430

Formatted by J.B. Fairfax Press Pty Limited
Printed by Toppan Printing Co, Singapore
PRINTED IN SINGAPORE

JBFP 348
Includes Index
ISBN 1 86343 186 1

DISTRIBUTION AND SALES
Australia: J.B. Fairfax Press Pty Limited
Ph: (02) 361 6366 Fax: (02) 360 6262
United Kingdom: J.B. Fairfax Press Limited
Ph (0933) 402330 Fax: (0933) 402234

ABOUT THIS BOOK

INGREDIENTS
Unless otherwise stated the following ingredients are used in this book:

Cream — Double, suitable for whipping
Flour — White flour, plain or standard
Sugar — White sugar

WHAT'S IN A TABLESPOON?
AUSTRALIA
1 tablespoon = 20 mL or 4 teaspoons
NEW ZEALAND
1 tablespoon = 15 mL or 3 teaspoons
UNITED KINGDOM
1 tablespoon = 15 mL or 3 teaspoons
The recipes in this book were tested in Australia where a 20 mL tablespoon is standard. The tablespoon in the New Zealand and the United Kingdom sets of measuring spoons is 15 mL. For recipes using baking powder, gelatine, bicarbonate of soda, small quantities of flour and cornflour, simply add another teaspoon for each tablespoon specified.

CANNED FOODS
Can sizes vary between countries and manufacturers. You may find the quantities in this book are slightly different to what is available. Purchase and use the can size nearest to the suggested size in the recipe.

MICROWAVE IT
Where microwave instructions occur in this book, a microwave oven with a 650 watt output has been used. Wattage on domestic microwave ovens varies between 500 and 700 watts, so it may be necessary to vary cooking times slightly depending on the wattage of your oven.

CONTENTS

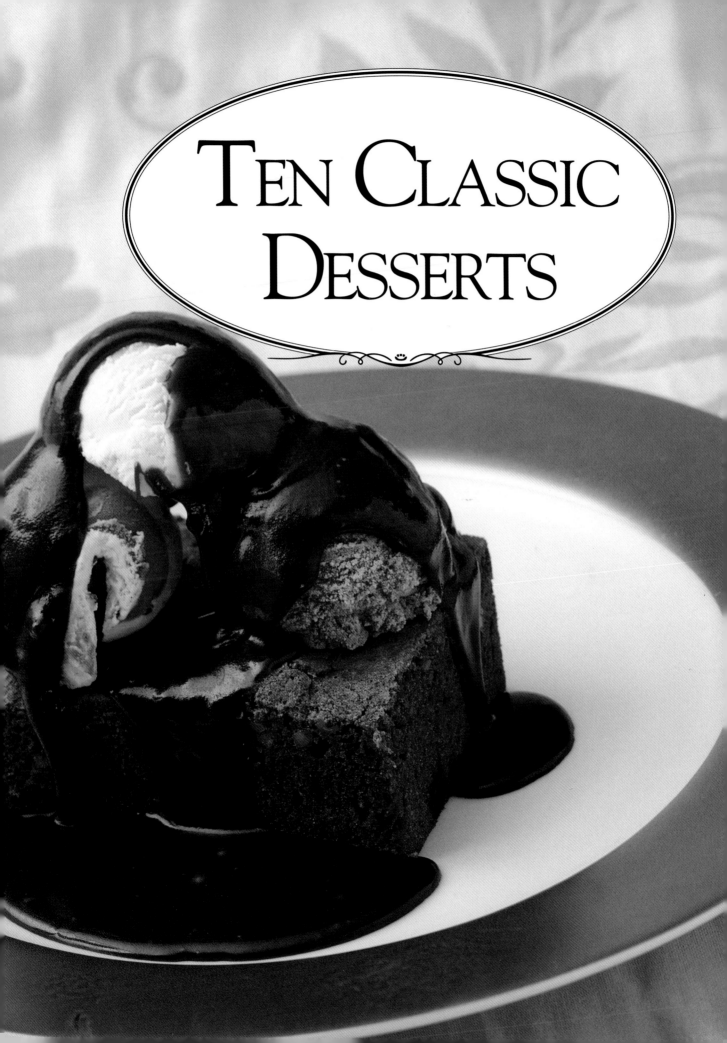

TEN CLASSIC DESSERTS

THE ULTIMATE CHOCOLATE SUNDAE

Oven temperature
180°C, 350°F, Gas 4

6 scoops vanilla ice cream
6 scoops chocolate ice cream
6 scoops choc chip ice cream

BROWNIE BASE
250 g/8 oz butter, melted
4 eggs, lightly beaten
1¹/₂ cups/330 g/10¹/₂ oz caster sugar
2 teaspoons vanilla essence
³/₄ cup/90 g/3 oz flour, sifted
¹/₄ cup/30 g/1 oz cocoa powder, sifted
60 g/2 oz chopped dates
45 g/1¹/₂ oz chopped pecans

FUDGE SAUCE
2 cups/350 g/11 oz brown sugar
¹/₄ cup/30 g/1 oz cocoa powder, sifted
1 cup/250 mL/8 fl oz cream (double)
2 tablespoons butter

1   To make base, place butter, eggs, caster sugar and vanilla essence in a bowl and beat to combine. Add flour, cocoa powder, dates and pecans and mix well to combine.

2   Pour mixture into a greased and lined 20 cm/8 in square cake tin and bake for 30 minutes or until firm to touch, but still fudgey in the centre. Cool in tin, then cut into six squares.

3   To make sauce, place brown sugar, cocoa powder, cream and butter in a saucepan and cook over a low heat, stirring constantly, until sugar dissolves. Bring to the boil, then reduce heat and simmer for 5 minutes or until sauce thickens slightly.

4   To assemble sundaes, top each brownie square with a scoop of vanilla, chocolate and choc chip ice cream. Drizzle with hot sauce and serve.

Extra fudge sauce can be stored in an airtight container in the refrigerator.

Serves 6

CHOCOLATE MOUSSE

300 g/9¹/₂ oz dark chocolate, broken into pieces
4 eggs, separated
100 g/3¹/₂ oz butter, softened
1 cup/250 mL/8 fl oz cream (double), whipped
1 tablespoon brandy
1 tablespoon sugar
white chocolate curls (optional)

1   Place chocolate in a heatproof bowl set over a saucepan of simmering water and heat, stirring, until chocolate melts. Remove bowl from pan and set aside to cool slightly.

2   Gradually beat egg yolks into chocolate. Add butter and beat until smooth. Fold in cream and brandy.

3   Place egg whites into a clean bowl and beat until soft peaks form. Gradually beat in sugar and continue beating until stiff peaks form. Fold egg white mixture into chocolate mixture.

4   Spoon mousse mixture into six dessert glasses and refrigerate until set. Decorate with chocolate curls, if desired.

To make chocolate curls, see instructions on page 79.

Serves 6

SACHER TORTE

250 g/8 oz butter, softened
1¹/₂ cups/265 g/8¹/₂ oz brown sugar
2 teaspoons vanilla essence
2 eggs, lightly beaten
1¹/₂ cups/185 g/6 oz flour
²/₃ cup/60 g/2 oz cocoa powder
³/₄ teaspoon baking powder
1¹/₂ cups/375 mL/8 fl oz buttermilk
¹/₂ cup/155 g/5 oz apricot jam

DARK CHOCOLATE ICING
185 g/6 oz dark chocolate, broken
into pieces
185 g/6 oz butter, chopped

1   Place butter, sugar and vanilla essence
in a bowl and beat until light and fluffy.
Gradually beat in eggs.

2   Sift together flour, cocoa powder and
baking powder over butter mixture. Add
buttermilk and mix well to combine.

3   Pour mixture into two greased and
lined 23 cm/9 in cake tins and bake for
25 minutes or until cakes are cooked
when tested with a skewer. Stand cakes in
tins for 5 minutes before turning onto
wire racks to cool.

4   To make icing, place chocolate and
butter in a heatproof bowl set over a
saucepan of simmering water and heat,
stirring, until mixture is smooth. Remove
bowl from pan and set aside to cool until
mixture thickens and is of a spreadable
consistency.

5   To assemble cake, place one cake on a
serving plate and spread with jam. Top
with remaining cake and spread top and
sides with icing. Place remaining icing in
a piping bag and pipe swirls around edge
of cake.

Serves 8-10

Oven temperature
180°C, 350°F, Gas 4

This Austrian favourite comes
complete with a hidden
layer of apricot jam. The
words 'Sacher Torte' piped
onto the top of the cake in
chocolate adds a touch of
authenticity to the decoration.

Previous pages: The Ultimate Chocolate
Sundae, Chocolate Mousse
Glasses Orrefors Kosta Boda *Fabric* Wardlaw
Right: Sacher Torte

Cake stand Villeroy & Boch *Fabric* Wardlaw

CHOCOLATE PROFITEROLES

Oven temperature
200°C, 400°F, Gas 6

185 g/6 oz dark chocolate, melted

CHOUX PASTRY
1 cup/250 mL/8 fl oz water
90 g/3 oz butter
1 cup/125 g/4 oz flour
3 eggs

CHOCOLATE LIQUEUR FILLING
$\frac{1}{2}$ cup/125 g/4 oz sugar
3 egg yolks
2 tablespoons flour
1 cup/250 mL/8 fl oz milk
60 g/2 oz dark chocolate, broken
into pieces
1 tablespoon orange-flavoured liqueur

1 To make pastry, place water and butter in a saucepan and slowly bring to the boil. As soon as the mixture boils, quickly stir in flour, using a wooden spoon. Cook over a low heat, stirring constantly, for 2 minutes or until mixture is smooth and leaves sides of pan.

2 Beat in eggs one at a time, beating well after each addition and until mixture is light and glossy.

3 Place heaped tablespoons of mixture on greased baking trays and bake for 10 minutes. Reduce oven temperature to 180°C/350°F/Gas 4 and cook for 10 minutes longer or until pastries are golden and crisp. Pierce a small hole in the base of each pastry and transfer to wire racks to cool.

4 To make filling, place sugar and egg yolks in a bowl and beat until thick and pale. Add flour and beat until combined.

5 Place milk, chocolate and liqueur in a a saucepan and heat over a medium heat, stirring constantly, until mixture is smooth. Remove pan from heat and slowly stir in egg yolk mixture. Return pan to heat and cook over medium heat, stirring constantly, until mixture thickens. Remove pan from heat, cover and set aside to cool.

6 Place filling in a piping bag fitted with a plain small nozzle and pipe filling through hole in base of profiteroles. Dip tops of profiteroles in melted chocolate and place on a wire rack to set.

Serves 6-8

Serve with whipped cream and fresh fruit. The pastry puffs can be baked in advance, cooled completely and stored in an airtight container at room temperature overnight or, for longer storage, in the freezer for up to six weeks, before filling.

Fabric Redelman & Son

CHOCOLATE ICE CREAM

Chocolate Profiteroles, Chocolate Ice Cream

1 cup/220 g/7 oz caster sugar
9 egg yolks
$^1/_2$ cup/45 g/$1^1/_2$ oz cocoa powder, sifted
2 cups/500 mL/16 fl oz milk
$2^1/_2$ cups/600 mL/1 pt cream (double)
125 g/4 oz milk chocolate, melted

1 Place sugar and egg yolks in a bowl and beat until thick and pale.

2 Place cocoa powder in a saucepan. Gradually stir in milk and cream and heat over a medium heat, stirring constantly, until mixture is almost boiling. Stir in chocolate.

3 Remove pan from heat and whisk hot milk mixture into egg mixture. Set aside to cool.

4 Pour mixture into a freezerproof container and freeze for 30 minutes or until mixture begins to freeze around edges. Beat mixture until even in texture. Return to freezer and repeat beating process two more times. Freeze until solid. Alternatively, place mixture in an ice cream maker and freeze according to manufacturer's instructions.

Serves 8

For true chocoholics, chopped chocolate or chocolate bits can be folded into the mixture before it freezes solid. Serve in scoops with vanilla tuiles or raspberries.

11

Chocolate Souffle

Oven temperature
190°C, 375°F, Gas 5

250 g/8 oz dark chocolate, broken
into pieces
1 cup/250 mL/8 fl oz cream (double)
6 eggs, separated
1 cup/220 g/7 oz caster sugar
$^1/_4$ cup/30 g/1 oz flour
icing sugar, sifted (optional)

To prepare soufflé dishes, brush interior of each with melted unsalted butter, coating lightly and evenly, then sprinkle lightly with caster sugar to coat.

1   Place chocolate and half the cream in a heatproof bowl set over a saucepan of simmering water and heat, stirring constantly, until mixture is smooth. Remove bowl from pan and set aside to cool slightly.

2   Place egg yolks and caster sugar in a clean bowl and beat until thick and pale.

Gradually beat in flour and remaining cream and beat until combined.

3   Transfer egg yolk mixture to a saucepan and cook over a medium heat, stirring constantly, for 5 minutes or until mixture thickens. Remove pan from heat and stir in chocolate mixture.

4   Place egg whites in a clean bowl and beat until stiff peaks form. Fold egg whites into chocolate mixture. Divide mixture evenly between six buttered and sugared 1 cup/250 mL/8 fl oz capacity soufflé dishes and bake for 25 minutes or until soufflés are puffed. Dust with icing sugar, if desired, and serve immediately.

Serves 6

BLACK FOREST GATEAU

200 g/6½ oz dark chocolate, chopped
3 cups/375 g/12 oz self-raising flour
1 cup/220 g/7 oz caster sugar
¼ cup/30 g/1 oz cocoa powder
1½ cups/375 mL/12 fl oz milk
3 eggs, lightly beaten
185 g/6 oz butter, softened
2 tablespoons cherry brandy
chocolate curls

CHERRY CREAM FILLING
2 cups/500 mL/16 fl oz cream (double)
⅓ cup/75 g/2½ oz caster sugar
440 g/14 oz canned pitted cherries, well
drained

1   Place chocolate in a heatproof bowl set over a saucepan of simmering water and heat, stirring, until chocolate melts. Remove bowl from pan and set aside to cool slightly.

2   Sift together flour, sugar and cocoa powder into a bowl. Add milk, eggs and butter and beat for 5 minutes or until mixture is smooth. Beat in chocolate until mixture is well combined.

3   Pour mixture into a greased, deep 23 cm/9 in round cake tin and bake for 60 minutes or until cake is cooked when tested with a skewer. Stand cake in tin for 5 minutes before turning onto a wire rack to cool.

4   To make filling, place cream and sugar in a bowl and beat until soft peaks form. Divide cream into two portions. Fold cherries into one portion.

5   To assemble cake, using a serrated edged knife, cut cake into three even layers. Sprinkle each layer with cherry brandy. Place one layer of cake on a serving plate, spread with half the cherry cream and top with a second layer of cake. Spread with remaining cherry cream and top with remaining layer of cake. Spread top and sides of cake with cream. Decorate top of cake with chocolate curls.

Serves 6-8

Oven temperature
180°C, 350°F, Gas 4

For even more sumptuous results, soak the cherries in extra cherry brandy or Kirsch overnight. Reserve a few cherries to decorate the top of the torte, then sprinkle all with a dusting of icing sugar just before serving.

Left: Chocolate Soufflé
Right: Black Forest Gâteau

THE BEST CHOCOLATE TORTE

Oven temperature
180°C, 350°F, Gas 4

155 g/5 oz dark chocolate, broken
into pieces
1 cup/170 g/5$\frac{1}{2}$ oz brown sugar
$\frac{1}{2}$ cup/125 mL/4 fl oz cream (double)
2 egg yolks
200 g/6$\frac{1}{2}$ oz butter, softened
1 cup/250 g/8 oz sugar
1 teaspoon vanilla essence
2 eggs, lightly beaten
1 cup/125 g/4 oz flour
1 cup/125 g/4 oz self-raising flour
$\frac{3}{4}$ cup/185 mL/6 fl oz milk
3 egg whites

RICH CHOCOLATE ICING
$\frac{3}{4}$ cup/185 g/6 oz sugar
$\frac{3}{4}$ cup/185 mL/6 fl oz water
6 egg yolks
200 g/6$\frac{1}{2}$ oz dark chocolate, melted
250 g/8 oz butter, chopped

DECORATIONS
90 g/3 oz flaked almonds, toasted
chocolate drizzled strawberries

1 Place chocolate, brown sugar, cream
and egg yolks in a heatproof bowl set over
a saucepan of simmering water and cook,
stirring constantly, until mixture is
smooth. Remove bowl from pan and set
aside to cool slightly.

2 Place butter, sugar and vanilla essence
in a bowl and beat until light and fluffy.
Gradually beat in eggs. Sift together flour
and self-raising flour over butter mixture.
Add chocolate mixture and milk and mix
until well combined.

3 Place egg whites in a clean bowl and
beat until stiff peaks form. Fold egg whites
into chocolate mixture. Pour mixture into
two greased and lined 23 cm/9 in round
cake tins and bake for 40 minutes or until
cakes are cooked when tested with a
skewer. Stand cakes in tins for 5 minutes
before turning onto wire racks to cool.

4 To make icing, place sugar and water
in saucepan and heat over a low heat,
stirring constantly, until sugar dissolves.
Bring to the boil, then reduce heat and
simmer for 4 minutes or until mixture is
syrupy.

5 Place egg yolks in a bowl and beat
until thick and pale. Gradually beat in
sugar syrup and melted chocolate. Then
gradually beat in butter and continue
beating until mixture is thick. Cover and
refrigerate until icing is of a spreadable
consistency.

6 To assemble torte, split each cake
horizontally. Place one layer of cake on a
serving plate and spread with icing. Top
with a second layer of cake and icing.
Repeat layers to use remaining cake.
Spread top and sides of cake with
remaining icing. Press almonds into sides
of torte and decorate top with chocolate
drizzled strawberries.

Serves 10-12

To prepare the strawberries,
wash, pat dry and place
berries on a tray. Pipe thin
lines of melted dark or white
chocolate back and forth
over the top and let stand
until set.

CHOCOLATE SELF-SAUCING PUDDING

Oven temperature
180°C, 350°F, Gas 4

1 cup/125 g/4 oz self-raising flour
$^1/_4$ cup/30 g/1 oz cocoa powder
$^3/_4$ cup/170 g/5$^1/_2$ oz caster sugar
$^1/_2$ cup/125 mL/4 fl oz milk
45 g/1$^1/_2$ oz butter, melted

CHOCOLATE SAUCE
$^3/_4$ cup/125 g/4 oz brown sugar
$^1/_4$ cup/30 g/1 oz cocoa powder, sifted
1$^1/_4$ cups/315 mL/10 fl oz hot water

1 Sift together flour and cocoa powder in a bowl. Add caster sugar and mix to combine. Make a well in the centre of the dry ingredients, add milk and butter and mix well to combine. Pour mixture into a greased 4 cup/1 litre/1$^3/_4$ pt capacity ovenproof dish.

2 To make sauce, place brown sugar and cocoa powder in a bowl. Gradually add water and mix until smooth. Carefully pour sauce over mixture in dish and bake for 40 minutes or until cake is cooked when tested with a skewer.

Serves 6

Serve scoops of pudding with some of the sauce from the base of the dish and top with a scoop of vanilla or chocolate ice cream.

Plate Waterford Wedgwood

Cake Stand Appley Hoare Fabric Wardlaw

RICH DEVIL'S FOOD CAKE

Left: Chocolate Self-Saucing Pudding
Above: Rich Devil's Food Cake

185 g/6 oz butter, softened
1³/₄ cups/375 g/12 oz caster sugar
3 eggs
2 cups/250 g/8 oz flour
²/₃ cup/60 g/2 oz cocoa powder
1¹/₂ teaspoons baking powder
1 cup/250 mL/8 fl oz milk
few drops red food colouring
icing sugar and extra cocoa
powder, sifted, for decorating

CHOCOLATE CREAM FILLING
¹/₂ cup/125 mL/4 fl oz cream (double)
90 g/3 oz dark chocolate, melted and
cooled
¹/₂ cup/155 g/5 oz raspberry jam

1   Place butter and caster sugar in a bowl
and beat until light and fluffy. Gradually
beat in eggs.

2   Sift together flour, cocoa powder and
baking powder over butter mixture. Add

milk and a few drops of food colouring
and mix well to combine. Pour mixture
into two greased and lined 20 cm/8 in
round cake tins and bake for 45 minutes
or until cakes are cooked when tested
with a skewer. Stand cakes in tins for 5
minutes before turning onto wire racks to
cool.

3   To make filling, place cream in a bowl
and beat until soft peaks form. Fold in
chocolate.

4   To assemble cake, place one cake on a
serving plate. Spread with jam and filling
and top with remaining cake. Just prior to
serving, dust top of cake with icing sugar.
From greaseproof paper, cut a template of
a devil's fork. Lay template on top of cake
and dust with cocoa powder.

Serves 8

Oven temperature
180°C, 350°F, Gas 4

It's the red food colouring
that gives this cake its
devilishly deep mahogany
hue.

17

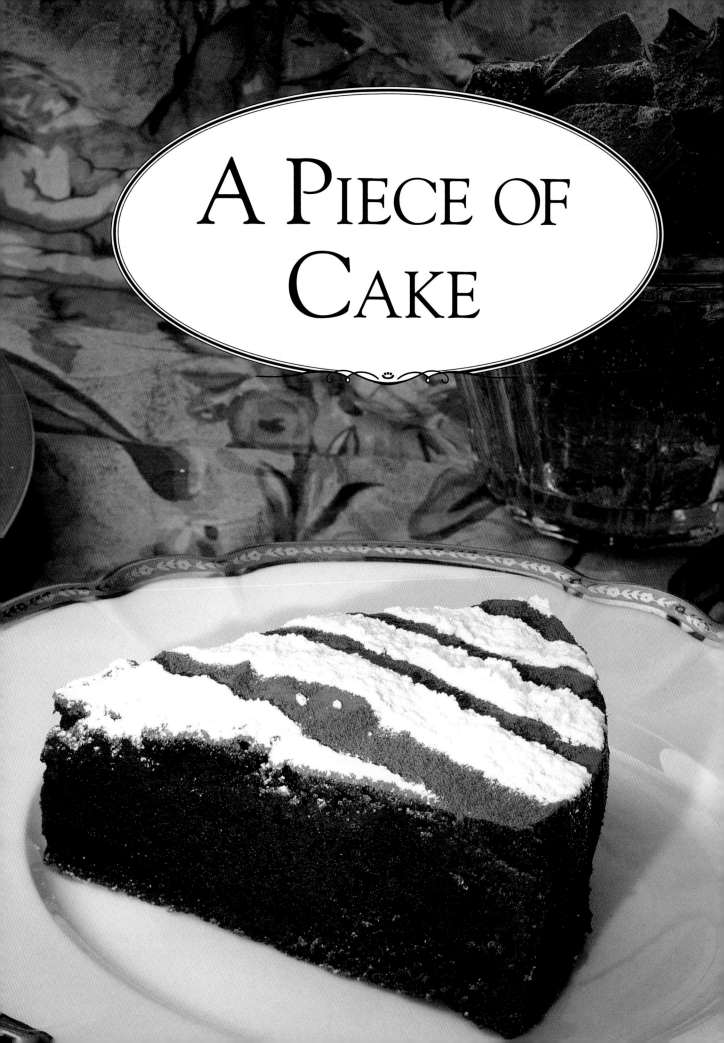

A PIECE OF CAKE

WHITE CHOCOLATE YOGURT CAKE

Oven temperature
180°C, 350°F, Gas 4

155 g/5 oz white chocolate, broken
into pieces
2 cups/250 g/8 oz self-raising flour
1 cup/220 g/7 oz caster sugar
2 eggs, lightly beaten
200 g/6$^1/_2$ oz natural yogurt
45 g/1$^1/_2$ oz butter, melted

WHITE CHOCOLATE ICING
75 g/2$^1/_2$ oz white chocolate
1 tablespoon cream (double)

Makes a 23 cm/9 in ring cake

1   Place chocolate in a heatproof bowl
set over a saucepan of simmering water
and heat, stirring, until smooth. Remove
bowl from pan and cool slightly.

2   Place flour, sugar, eggs, yogurt and
butter in a bowl and beat for 5 minutes
or until mixture is smooth. Add melted
chocolate and mix well to combine.

3   Pour mixture into a greased
23 cm/9 in ring tin and bake for
50 minutes or until cake is cooked when
tested with a skewer. Stand cake in tin for
5 minutes before turning onto a wire rack
to cool.

4   To make icing, place chocolate and
cream in a heatproof bowl set over a
saucepan of simmering water and heat,
stirring, until mixture is smooth. Spread
icing over top and sides of cake.

BEST MUD CAKE

Oven temperature
180°C, 350°F, Gas 4

Serve cake in wedges with
cream. For a decorative
touch, place a paper doily
on top of cake before
dusting with the cocoa
powder or icing sugar, then
carefully lift off the paper to
reveal the pattern.

*Previous pages: Best Mud Cake,
White Chocolate Yogurt Cake*
Plates Limoges Australia *Fabric* Wardlaw
Right: Individual Dessert Cakes

350 g/11 oz dark chocolate, broken
into pieces
$^3/_4$ cup/170 g/5$^1/_2$ oz caster sugar
185 g/6 oz butter, chopped
5 eggs, separated
$^1/_3$ cup/45 g/1$^1/_2$ oz flour, sifted
cocoa powder, sifted
icing sugar, sifted

Makes a 23 cm/9 in round cake

1   Place chocolate, caster sugar and
butter in a heatproof bowl set over a
saucepan of simmering water and heat,
stirring, until mixture is smooth. Remove
bowl and set aside to cool slightly. Beat in
egg yolks one at a time, beating well after
each addition. Fold in flour.

2   Place egg whites in a clean bowl and
beat until stiff peaks form. Fold egg whites
into chocolate mixture. Pour mixture into
a greased 23 cm/9 in springform tin and
bake for 45 minutes or until cake is
cooked when tested with a skewer. Cool
cake in tin.

3   Just prior to serving dust cake with
cocoa powder and icing sugar.

INDIVIDUAL DESSERT CAKES

100 g/3¹/₂ oz dark chocolate, broken
into pieces
125 g/4 oz butter, chopped
2 egg yolks
2 eggs
¹/₃ cup/90 g/3 oz sugar
2 tablespoons flour
cocoa powder, sifted

Serves 6

1   Place chocolate and butter in a heatproof bowl set over a saucepan of simmering water and heat, stirring, until mixture is smooth. Remove bowl from pan and set aside to cool.

2   Place egg yolks, eggs and sugar in a bowl and beat until thick and pale. Gradually beat in flour and chocolate mixture and beat well. Divide mixture evenly between six greased small fluted brioche moulds or small ramekins, place on a baking tray and bake for 12-15 minutes or until cakes are just firm – the centres should still be soft and fudgey. Turn onto serving plates and dust with cocoa powder.

Oven temperature
180°C, 350°F, Gas 4

Delicious served with spiced mascarpone or ice cream and chocolate sauce. To make spiced mascarpone, fold 1 tablespoon finely chopped crystallised ginger, 1 tablespoon honey and ground mixed spice to taste into 375 g/12 oz mascarpone. Chill until ready to serve.

Plate Villeroy & Boch

CHOCOLATE POUND CAKE

Oven temperature
190°C, 375°F, Gas 5

This rich buttery cake can be served plain, with a purchased chocolate sauce or with cream. A simple glacé icing drizzled over the top makes another delicious alternative.

185 g/6 oz butter, softened
1$\frac{1}{2}$ cups/330 g/10$\frac{1}{2}$ oz caster sugar
3 teaspoons vanilla essence
3 eggs, lightly beaten
1$\frac{1}{2}$ cups/185 g/6 oz self-raising flour
$\frac{1}{2}$ cup/60 g/2 oz flour
$\frac{1}{2}$ cup/45 g/1$\frac{1}{2}$ oz cocoa powder
1$\frac{1}{4}$ cups/315 mL/10 fl oz milk

1 Place butter, sugar and vanilla essence in a bowl and beat until light and fluffy. Gradually beat in eggs.

2 Sift together self-raising flour, flour and cocoa powder. Fold flour mixture and milk, alternately, into butter mixture.

3 Pour mixture into a greased and lined 20 cm/8 in square cake tin and bake for 55 minutes or until cake is cooked when tested with a skewer. Stand cake in tin for 10 minutes before turning onto a wire rack to cool.

Makes a 20 cm/8 in square cake

GRANDMA'S CHOCOLATE CAKE

125 g/4 oz butter, softened
2 cups/440 g/14 oz caster sugar
2 eggs
2 teaspoons vanilla essence
1 cup/125 g/4 oz self-raising flour
³/₄ cup/90 g/3 oz flour
³/₄ cup/75 g/2¹/₂ oz cocoa powder
1 cup/250 mL/8 fl oz buttermilk

CHOCOLATE SOUR CREAM FILLING

185 g/6 oz dark chocolate, broken into pieces
125 g/4 oz butter, chopped
3¹/₄ cups/500 g/1 lb icing sugar, sifted
¹/₂ cup/125 g/4 oz sour cream
³/₄ cup/235 g/7¹/₂ oz raspberry jam

1 Place butter, caster sugar, eggs and vanilla essence in a bowl and beat until light and fluffy. Sift together self-raising flour, flour and cocoa powder.

2 Fold flour mixture and milk, alternately, into butter mixture. Divide mixture between four greased and lined 23 cm/9 in round cake tins and bake for 25 minutes or until cakes are cooked when tested with a skewer. Turn cakes onto wire racks to cool.

3 To make filling, place chocolate and butter in a heatproof bowl set over a saucepan of simmering water and heat, stirring, until mixture is smooth. Remove bowl from pan. Add icing sugar and sour cream and mix until smooth.

4 To assemble cake, place one cake on a serving plate and spread with some jam and top with some filling. Top with a second cake, some more jam and filling. Repeat layers to use all cakes and jam. Finish with a layer of cake and spread remaining filling over top and sides of cake.

Makes a 23 cm/9 in round cake

Oven temperature
180°C, 350°F, Gas 4

When buttermilk is unavailable, substitute with sour milk prepared by placing 1 tablespoon white or cider vinegar in a measuring jug and adding enough fresh milk to measure the amount of buttermilk required. Stand this mixture at room temperature for 15-20 minutes or until curdled.

Left: Chocolate Pound Cake
Right: Grandma's Chocolate Cake

Plate Limoges Australia Glass Appley Hoare Fabric Wardlaw

CHOCOLATE ESPRESSO CHEESECAKE

Oven temperature
200°C, 400°F, Gas 6

250 g/8 oz chocolate wafer biscuits,
crushed
155 g/5 oz butter, melted

CHOCOLATE ESPRESSO FILLING
2 tablespoons instant espresso
coffee powder
1 tablespoon hot water
250 g/8 oz cream cheese, softened
1 cup/250 g/8 oz sour cream
3 eggs, lightly beaten
1 cup/250 g/8 oz sugar
155 g/5 oz dark chocolate, melted

COFFEE LIQUEUR GLAZE
1/4 cup/60 mL/2 fl oz coffee-flavoured
liqueur
1/4 cup/60 mL/2 fl oz rum
250 g/8 oz dark chocolate, broken
into pieces
60 g/2 oz butter
1/2 cup/125 mL/4 fl oz cream (double)

To prevent the cheesecake
from cracking as it cools,
bake until a knife inserted just
off centre comes out clean,
then place cake in a
draught-free place or in the
turned-off oven with the door
ajar until cooled completely.

1   To make base, place biscuit crumbs
and butter in a bowl and mix to combine.
Press mixture over the base of a lightly
greased and lined 20 cm/8 in springform
tin. Refrigerate until firm.

2   To make filling, place coffee powder
and water in a bowl and mix until coffee
powder dissolves. Set aside to cool slightly.

3   Place cream cheese, sour cream, eggs,
sugar and coffee mixture in a bowl and
beat until smooth.

4   Pour half the filling over prepared
base. Drop 4 tablespoons of melted
chocolate into filling and swirl with a
skewer. Repeat with remaining filling and
chocolate and bake for 40 minutes or
until cheesecake is firm. Cool in tin.

5   To make glaze, place liqueur and rum
into a saucepan and bring to simmering
over a medium heat. Simmer, stirring
occasionally, until mixture reduces to
1/4 cup/60 mL/2 fl oz. Add chocolate,
butter and cream and cook, stirring, until
mixture is smooth. Remove pan from
heat and set aside until mixture thickens
slightly. Spread glaze over cheesecake and
allow to set.

Serves 10

CHOCOLATE HAZELNUT TORTE

Oven temperature
190°C, 375°F, Gas 5

To toast hazelnuts, place nuts
on a baking tray and bake
for 10 minutes or until skins
begin to split. Place nuts on a
teatowel and rub to remove
skins. Place nuts in a food
processor and process to
roughly chop.

*Chocolate Espresso Cheesecake,
Chocolate Hazelnut Torte*

250 g/8 oz dark chocolate, broken
into pieces
6 eggs, separated
1 cup/250 g/8 oz sugar
315 g/10 oz hazelnuts, toasted and
roughly chopped
1 tablespoon rum
icing sugar, sifted

1   Place chocolate in a heatproof bowl set
over a saucepan of simmering water and
heat, stirring, until chocolate melts.
Remove bowl from pan and cool slightly.

2   Place egg yolks and sugar in a bowl and
beat until thick and pale. Fold chocolate,
hazelnuts and rum into egg mixture.

3   Place egg whites into a clean bowl and
beat until stiff peaks form. Fold egg whites
into chocolate mixture. Pour mixture into
a greased and lined 23 cm/9 in springform
tin and bake for 50 minutes or until cake
is cooked when tested with a skewer.
Cool cake in tin. Just prior to serving dust
cake with icing sugar.

Serves 8

Above: Chocolate Pecan Gâteau
Right: Simple Chocolate Cake

CHOCOLATE PECAN GATEAU

Oven temperature
160°C, 325°F, Gas 3

4 eggs, separated
³/₄ cup/170 g/5¹/₂ oz caster sugar
2 tablespoons brandy
200 g/6¹/₂ oz pecans, roughly chopped
2 tablespoons flour

CHOCOLATE BRANDY GLAZE
315 g/10 oz milk chocolate
2 teaspoons instant coffee powder
¹/₃ cup/90 mL/3 fl oz cream (double)
1 tablespoon brandy
155 g/5 oz pecans, roughly chopped

Apply nut garnish while the glaze is still slightly tacky. Hold the gâteau on its base in the palm of one hand and tilt over a plate of the nuts. Scoop the nuts with your free hand and press carefully against the sides of the gâteau. Rotate gâteau and continue to press nuts around the sides until evenly coated.

Serves 8

1   Place egg yolks, sugar and brandy in a bowl and beat until thick and pale. Place egg whites in a clean bowl and beat until stiff peaks form. Fold egg whites, pecans and flour into egg yolk mixture.

2   Pour mixture into a lightly greased and lined 23 cm/9 in springform tin and bake for 40 minutes or until cake is firm. Cool in tin.

3   To make glaze, place chocolate, coffee powder, cream and brandy in a heatproof bowl set over a saucepan of simmering water and heat, stirring, until mixture is smooth. Remove bowl from pan and set aside to cool slightly. Spread glaze over top and sides of cooled cake. Sprinkle pecans over top of cake and press into side of cake. Allow to set before serving.

SIMPLE CHOCOLATE CAKE

125 g/4 oz butter, softened
1 cup/250 g/8 oz sugar
1 teaspoon vanilla essence
2 eggs, lightly beaten
1¼ cups/155 g/5 oz self-raising flour
½ cup/45 g/1½ oz cocoa powder
1 teaspoon bicarbonate of soda
1 cup/250 mL/8 fl oz milk
gold or silver dragees

CHOCOLATE BUTTER ICING
125 g/4 oz dark chocolate
60 g/2 oz butter
¼ cup/60 mL/2 fl oz cream (double)

1   Place butter, sugar and vanilla essence in a bowl and beat until light and fluffy. Gradually beat in eggs.

2   Sift flour, cocoa powder and bicarbonate of soda together into a bowl.

Fold flour mixture and milk alternately into egg mixture.

3   Pour mixture into a greased and lined 18 cm/7 in square cake tin and bake for 40 minutes or until cake is cooked when tested with a skewer. Stand cake in tin for 5 minutes before turning onto a wire rack to cool.

4   To make icing, place chocolate, butter and cream in a heatproof bowl set over a saucepan of simmering water and heat, stirring constantly, until mixture is smooth. Remove bowl from pan and set aside to cool slightly. Spread top and sides of cake with icing and decorate with gold or silver dragees.

Makes an 18 cm/7 in square cake

Oven temperature
180°C, 350°F, Gas 4

This basic butter cake is a good one for baking in muffin or patty tins for individual servings in school or office lunch boxes. Fill tins two-thirds full with batter and bake until cooked when tested with a skewer. Drizzle with a simple glacé icing when cold.

Plate Appley Hoare

THE BISCUIT
BARREL

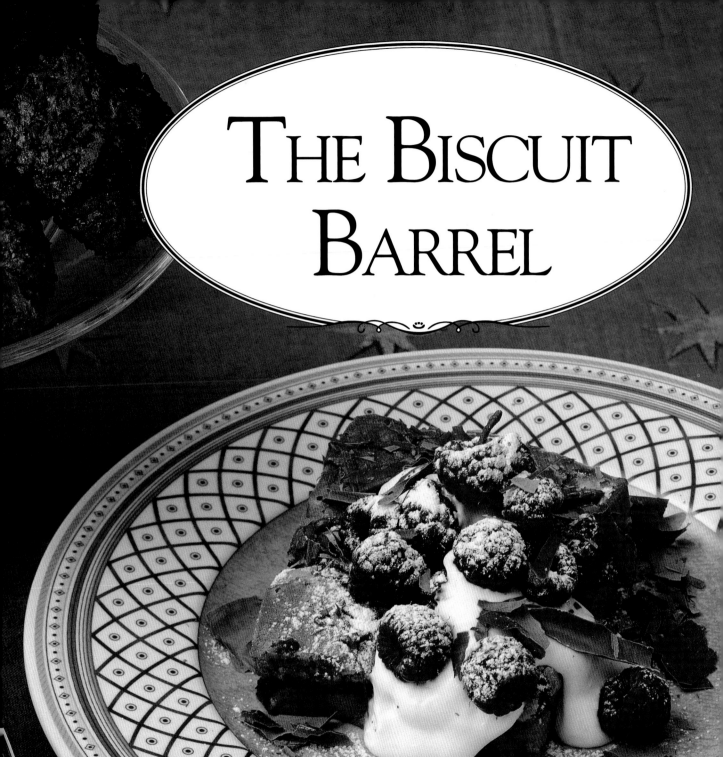

NIGHT SKY COOKIES

Oven temperature
190°C, 375°F, Gas 5

125 g/4 oz butter, softened
$^3/_4$ cup/170 g/5$^1/_2$ oz caster sugar
$^1/_2$ teaspoon almond essence
1 egg, lightly beaten
2 cups/250 g/8 oz flour
$^1/_2$ teaspoon baking powder
$^1/_4$ cup/60 mL/2 fl oz milk
125 g/4 oz dark chocolate, melted
90 g/3 oz white chocolate, melted

1   Place butter, sugar and almond essence in a bowl and beat until light and fluffy. Gradually beat in egg.

2   Sift together flour and baking powder. Fold flour mixture and milk, alternately, into butter mixture and mix to form a soft dough.

3   Roll out dough on a lightly floured surface to 5 mm/$^1/_4$ in thick. Using a star and a moon-shaped cookie cutter, cut out cookies. Place cookies on lightly greased baking trays and bake for 10 minutes or until cookies are golden and cooked. Transfer to wire racks to cool.

4   Dip tops of moon-shaped cookies in white chocolate and tips of star-shaped cookies in dark chocolate. Place on wire racks to set.

Makes 24

CHOCOLATE MACAROONS

Oven temperature
180°C, 350°F, Gas 4

Avoid baking these on a humid day as moisture will affect their texture. Store macaroons in an airtight container in a cool, dry place.

2 egg whites
$^3/_4$ cup/170 g/5$^1/_2$ oz caster sugar
$^1/_2$ cup/45 g/1$^1/_2$ oz cocoa powder, sifted
1$^1/_2$ cups/140 g/4$^1/_2$ oz shredded coconut

1   Place egg whites in a bowl and beat until stiff peaks form. Gradually beat in sugar and continue beating until mixture is thick and glossy.

2   Fold cocoa powder and coconut into egg whites. Drop tablespoons of mixture onto greased baking trays and bake for 15 minutes or until macaroons are firm. Transfer to wire racks to cool.

Makes 20

Previous pages: Chocolate Macaroons, White Choc and Raspberry Slice (page 32), Night Sky Cookies
Plates Villeroy & Boch *Fabric* Wardlaw
Right: Double Fudge Blondies

DOUBLE FUDGE BLONDIES

250 g/8 oz butter, softened
1¹/₂ cups/375 g/12 oz sugar
1 teaspoon vanilla essence
4 eggs, lightly beaten
1³/₄ cups/220 g/7 oz flour
¹/₂ teaspoon baking powder
185 g/6 oz white chocolate, melted

CREAM CHEESE FILLING
250 g/8 oz cream cheese, softened
60 g/2 oz white chocolate, melted
¹/₄ cup/60 mL/2 fl oz maple syrup
1 egg
1 tablespoon flour

1   To make filling, place cream cheese, chocolate, maple syrup, egg and flour in a bowl and beat until smooth. Set aside.

2   Place butter, sugar and vanilla essence in a bowl and beat until light and fluffy. Gradually beat in eggs.

3   Sift together flour and baking powder over butter mixture. Add chocolate and mix well to combine.

4   Spread half the mixture over the base of a greased and lined 23 cm/9 in square cake tin. Top with filling and remaining mixture. Bake for 40 minutes or until firm. Cool in tin, then cut into squares.

Makes 24

Oven temperature
180°C, 350°F, Gas 4

These lusciously rich white brownies can double as a dinner party dessert if drizzled with melted white or dark chocolate and topped with toasted flaked almonds.

Fabric Wardlaw

WHITE CHOC AND RASPBERRY SLICE

Oven temperature
160°C, 325°F, Gas 3

250 g/8 oz butter, softened
1¹/₂ cups/375 g/12 oz sugar
³/₄ cup/125 g/4 oz brown sugar
1 teaspoon vanilla essence
4 eggs, lightly beaten
200 g/6¹/₂ oz white chocolate, melted
1¹/₂ cups/185 g/6 oz flour, sifted
315 g/10 oz fresh or frozen raspberries

BRANDY CHOCOLATE GLAZE
100 g/3¹/₂ oz milk chocolate
2 tablespoons brandy
2 teaspoons hot water

Serve as a special treat for afternoon tea with a dollop of brandy-flavoured whipped cream and additional berries, if desired.

1   Place butter, sugar, brown sugar and vanilla essence in a bowl and beat until light and fluffy. Gradually beat in eggs. Add white chocolate and beat well.

2   Add flour to chocolate mixture and mix to combine. Pour mixture into a greased and lined 18 x 28 cm/7 x 11 in shallow cake tin. Sprinkle with raspberries and bake for 30 minutes or until base is firm. Cool in tin.

3   To make glaze, place milk chocolate in a heatproof bowl set over a saucepan of simmering water and heat, stirring, until chocolate melts. Stir in brandy and water and mix well to combine.

4   Drizzle glaze over slice and allow glaze to set before cutting into bars.

Makes 28

CHOC MINT PINWHEELS

Oven temperature
200°C, 400°F, Gas 6

100 g/3¹/₂ oz butter, softened
³/₄ cup/170 g/5¹/₂ oz caster sugar
1 egg, lightly beaten
1¹/₂ cups/185 g/6 oz flour
1 teaspoon peppermint essence
2 tablespoons cocoa powder

You may want to add a few drops of green or pink food colouring to the mint-flavoured dough. Chill the rolled dough until quite firm for easier slicing.

1   Place butter and sugar in a bowl and beat until light and fluffy. Gradually beat in egg. Add flour and mix to make a soft dough.

2   Divide dough into two equal portions. Knead peppermint essence into one portion and cocoa powder into the other. Roll out each portion of dough separately on nonstick baking paper to make an 18 x 28 cm/7 x 11 in rectangle. Place peppermint dough on top of chocolate dough. Roll up from long edge, wrap roll in plastic food wrap and chill for 1 hour.

3   Cut roll into 5 mm/¹/₄ in thick slices and place on greased baking trays. Bake for 8 minutes or until cookies are golden. Transfer to wire racks to cool.

Makes 40

Plate and jar Appley Hoare

WHITE CHOC HAZELNUT COOKIES

White Choc Hazelnut Cookies, Choc Mint Pinwheels

2 cups/500 g/1 lb chocolate hazelnut spread
125 g/4 oz butter, softened
2 cups/350 g/11 oz brown sugar
1 tablespoon vanilla essence
3 eggs, lightly beaten
1¾ cups/220 g/7 oz flour
2 teaspoons baking powder
185 g/6 oz hazelnuts, toasted, roughly chopped
250 g/8 oz white chocolate, chopped

1   Place chocolate hazelnut spread, butter, sugar and vanilla essence in a bowl and beat until thick and creamy. Gradually beat in eggs.

2   Sift together flour and baking powder. Fold flour mixture into butter mixture. Add hazelnuts and chocolate and mix to combine.

3   Drop tablespoons of mixture onto greased baking trays and bake for 10 minutes or until cookies are golden. Transfer to wire racks to cool.

Makes 24

Oven temperature
180°C, 350°F, Gas 4

If desired, pipe additional chocolate hazelnut spread in thin lines across the top of these biscuits to decorate before serving.

MOCHA TRUFFLE COOKIES

Oven temperature
180°C, 350°F, Gas 4

125 g/4 oz butter, chopped
90 g/3 oz dark chocolate, broken
into pieces
2 tablespoons instant espresso coffee
powder
2¹/₂ cups/315 g/10 oz flour
¹/₂ cup/45 g/1¹/₂ oz cocoa powder
1 teaspoon baking powder
2 eggs, lightly beaten
1 cup/250 g/8 oz sugar
1 cup/170 g/5¹/₂ oz brown sugar
2 teaspoons vanilla essence
125 g/4 oz pecans, chopped

1   Place butter, chocolate and coffee powder in a heatproof bowl set over a saucepan of simmering water and heat, stirring, until mixture is smooth. Remove bowl from pan and set aside to cool slightly.

2   Sift together flour, cocoa powder and baking powder into a bowl. Add eggs, sugar, brown sugar, vanilla essence and chocolate mixture and mix well to combine. Stir in pecans.

3   Drop tablespoons of mixture onto greased baking trays and bake for 12 minutes or until puffed. Stand cookies on trays for 2 minutes before transferring to wire racks to cool.

This is the biscuit version of the traditional rich truffle confection and tastes delicious as an after-dinner treat with coffee.

Makes 40

CHOC LAYER BISCUITS

Oven temperature
180°C, 350°F, Gas 4

250 g/8 oz butter
1 cup/170 g/5¹/₂ oz brown sugar
³/₄ cup/185 g/6 oz sugar
2 teaspoons vanilla essence
1 egg
2³/₄ cups/350g/11 oz flour
1 teaspoon baking powder
¹/₂ cup/45 g/1¹/₂ oz cocoa powder
¹/₂ cup/45 g/1¹/₂ oz malted milk powder

1   Place butter, brown sugar, sugar and vanilla essence in a bowl and beat until light and fluffy. Add egg and beat well. Sift together flour and baking powder. Add flour mixture to butter mixture and mix to make a soft dough.

2   Divide dough into two equal portions. Knead cocoa powder into one portion and malted milk powder into the other.

3   Roll out each portion of dough separately on nonstick baking paper to make a 20 x 30 cm/8 x 12 in rectangle. Place chocolate dough on top of malt dough and press together.

4   Cut in half lengthwise and place one layer of dough on top of the other. You should now have four layers of dough in alternating colours. Place layered dough on a tray, cover with plastic food wrap and chill for 1 hour.

5   Cut dough into 1 cm/¹/₂ in wide fingers and place on greased baking trays. Bake for 15 minutes or until biscuits are golden and crisp. Transfer to wire racks to cool.

Makes 40

For a special occasion, dip the ends of cooled biscuits into melted white or dark chocolate and place on a wire rack until chocolate sets.

Mocha Truffle Cookies, Choc Layer Biscuits

ORIGINAL CHOC CHIP COOKIES

Oven temperature
180°C, 350°F, Gas 4

Everyone's favourite biscuit, full of the flavour of coconut, toasted hazelnuts and a generous portion of chocolate chips!

250 g/8 oz butter, softened
1 cup/170 g/5¹⁄₂ oz brown sugar
1 egg
1¹⁄₂ cups/185 g/6 oz self-raising flour
¹⁄₂ cup/60 g/2 oz flour
45 g/1¹⁄₂ oz desiccated coconut
220 g/7 oz chocolate chips
185 g/6 oz hazelnuts, toasted, roughly chopped

1   Place butter and sugar in a bowl and beat until light and fluffy. Beat in egg.

2   Add self-raising flour, flour, coconut, chocolate chips and hazelnuts to butter mixture and mix to combine.

3   Drop tablespoons of mixture onto greased baking trays and bake for 12-15 minutes or until cookies are golden. Transfer to wire racks to cool.

Makes 35

Jar Appley Hoare Fabric Wardlaw

36

Plates Waterford Wedgwood Fabric Wardlaw

DOUBLE CHOC BROWNIES

Left: Original Choc Chip Cookies
Above: Double Choc Brownies

1¹/₂ cups/375 g/12 oz sugar
200 g/6¹/₂ oz dark chocolate, melted
1 cup/250 mL/8 fl oz vegetable oil
2 teaspoons vanilla essence
4 eggs
1³/₄ cups/220 g/7 oz flour
1 teaspoon baking powder

CHOCOLATE GLAZE
185 g/6 oz dark chocolate
2 teaspoons vegetable oil

1   Place sugar, chocolate, oil, vanilla essence and eggs in a bowl and whisk to combine. Sift together flour and baking powder. Add flour mixture to chocolate mixture and mix well to combine.

2   Pour mixture into a greased and lined 20 cm/8 in square cake tin and bake for 40 minutes or until firm to touch. Cool in tin, then cut into 5 cm/2 in squares and place on a wire rack.

3   To make glaze, place chocolate in a heatproof bowl set over a saucepan of simmering water and heat, stirring, until chocolate melts. Stir in oil. Spoon glaze over brownies and stand until set.

Makes 20

Oven temperature
180°C, 350°F, Gas 4

These intensely chocolatey and tender treats will stay moist and delicious for several days if stored in an airtight container in a cool, dry place.

37

CHOCKY ROAD BISCUITS

Oven temperature
180°C, 350°F, Gas 4

250 g/8 oz butter, softened
1 cup/170 g/5^1/$_2$ oz brown sugar
2 eggs, lightly beaten
3 cups/375 g/12 oz flour
1 cup/100 g/3^1/$_2$ oz cocoa powder
^{1}/$_4$ cup/60 mL/2 fl oz buttermilk or milk
155 g/5 oz white chocolate, roughly
chopped
90 g/3 oz dry roasted peanuts
185 g/6 oz chocolate chips

1   Place butter and sugar in a bowl and beat until light and fluffy. Gradually beat in eggs.

2   Sift together flour and cocoa powder. Add flour mixture, milk, chocolate, peanuts and chocolate chips to egg mixture and mix well to combine.

3   Drop tablespoons of mixture onto lightly greased baking trays and bake for 10 minutes or until biscuits are cooked. Transfer to wire racks to cool.

Makes 36

Marshmallows, peanuts and chocolate chips must be the three most favourite additions to any biscuit designed for kids.

CRAZY COOKIES

Oven temperature
180°C, 350°F, Gas 4

75 g/2^1/$_2$ oz milk chocolate
220 g/7 oz butter, softened
1 cup/220 g/7 oz caster sugar
1^1/$_2$ cups/185 g/6 oz self-raising flour
60 g/2 oz hundreds and thousands
coated chocolates
60 g/2 oz caramel whirls

1   Place chocolate in a heatproof bowl set over a saucepan of simmering water and heat, stirring, until smooth. Remove bowl from pan and set aside to cool slightly.

2   Place butter and sugar in a bowl and beat until light and fluffy. Add flour and chocolate to butter mixture and mix well to combine.

3   Roll tablespoons of mixture into balls and place on lightly greased baking trays. Flatten slightly and press a chocolate or a caramel whirl into the centre of each cookie. Bake for 12 minutes or until cookies are firm. Transfer to wire racks to cool.

Makes 36

A buttery shortbread biscuit base is the perfect foil for sweet confectionery decorations.

Chocky Road Biscuits, Crazy Cookies

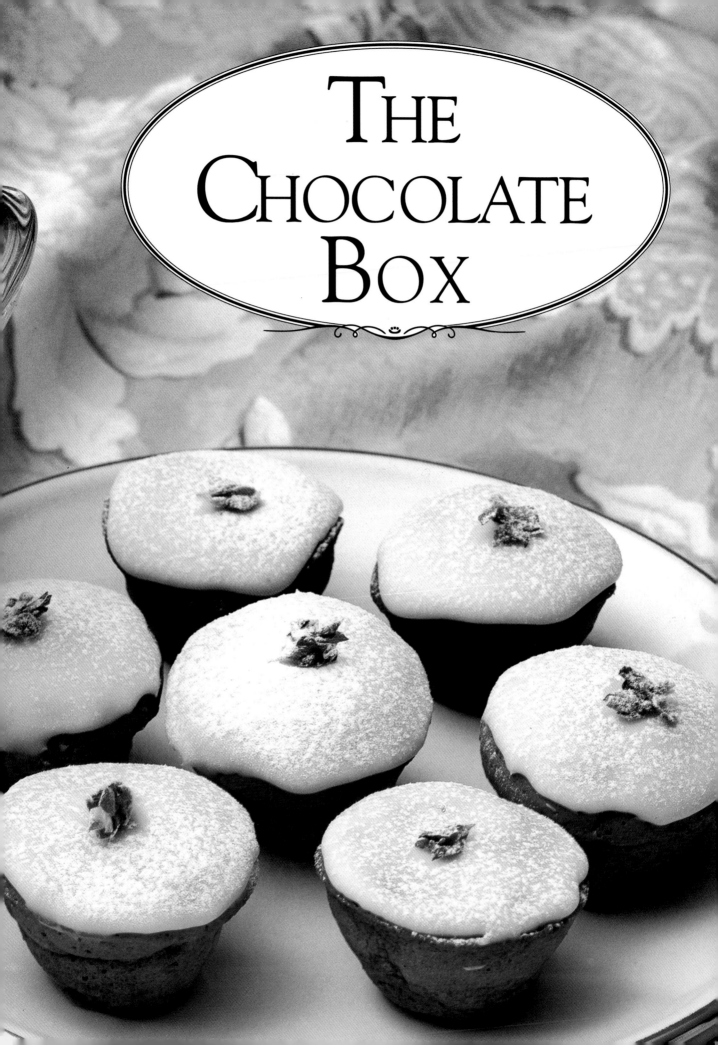

THE
CHOCOLATE
BOX

HAZELNUT SNOWBALLS

200 g/6¹/₂ oz white chocolate, broken into pieces
45 g/1¹/₂ oz butter, chopped
¹/₄ cup/60 mL/2 fl oz cream (double)
1 tablespoon hazelnut-flavoured liqueur (optional)
125 g/4 oz hazelnuts, toasted, skins removed
60 g/2 oz desiccated coconut

To toast hazelnuts refer to tip on page 24. You may also wish to toast the coconut used for rolling, for a richer flavour.

1 Place chocolate, butter, cream and liqueur, if using, in a heatproof bowl set over a saucepan of simmering water and heat, stirring, until mixture is smooth. Remove bowl from pan and set aside to cool slightly.

2 Stir chocolate mixture until thick and pliable. Roll tablespoons of mixture into balls. Press a hazelnut into the centre of each ball and roll to enclose nut. Roll balls in coconut and refrigerate for 1 hour or until firm.

Makes 40

CHOCOLATE FIG TRUFFLES

185 g/6 oz milk chocolate, broken into pieces
90 g/3 oz butter, chopped
¹/₂ cup/125 mL/4 fl oz cream (double)
¹/₄ cup/60 mL/2 fl oz light corn syrup or golden syrup
1 tablespoon cognac or brandy
75 g/2¹/₂ oz chopped dried figs
45 g/1¹/₂ oz slivered almonds, toasted
60 g/2 oz flaked almonds, toasted

If preferred, chopped soft dried prunes or dates may be used in place of the figs.

1 Place chocolate, butter, cream, corn or golden syrup and cognac or brandy in a heatproof bowl set over a saucepan of simmering water and heat, stirring, until mixture is smooth. Remove bowl from pan.

2 Add figs and slivered almonds to chocolate mixture and mix well to combine. Chill mixture for 1 hour or until firm enough to roll into balls.

3 Take 3 teaspoons of mixture and roll into balls, then roll in flaked almonds. Place on nonstick baking paper and chill until required.

Makes 24

*Previous pages: Tiny Fudge Cakes (page 44), Hazelnut Snowballs, Chocolate Fig Truffles
Right: Choc Almond Biscotti*

CHOC ALMOND BISCOTTI

2 cups/250 g/8 oz flour
³/₄ cup/75 g/2¹/₂ oz cocoa powder
1 teaspoon bicarbonate of soda
1 cup/250 g/8 oz sugar
200 g/6¹/₂ oz blanched almonds
2 eggs
1 egg yolk

Makes 35

1   Sift together flour, cocoa powder and bicarbonate of soda into a bowl. Make a well in the centre of the flour mixture, add sugar, almonds and eggs and mix well to form a soft dough.

2   Turn dough onto a lightly floured surface and knead until smooth. Divide dough into four equal portions. Roll out each portion of dough to make a strip that is 5 mm/¹/₄ in thick and 4 cm/1¹/₂ in wide.

3   Place strips on a baking tray lined with nonstick baking paper. Brush with egg yolk and bake for 30 minutes or until lightly browned. Cut strips into 1 cm/¹/₂ in slices, return to baking tray and bake for 10 minutes longer or until dry.

Oven temperature
180°C, 350°F, Gas 4

Biscuits may be partially dipped into melted chocolate for a two-toned effect. Before the chocolate sets completely, dip into toasted crushed almonds.

Glass dish Appley Hoare Fabric Wardlaw

TINY FUDGE CAKES

Oven temperature
180°C, 350°F, Gas 4

100 g/3¹/₂ oz dark chocolate
60 g/2 oz butter
3 eggs, separated
¹/₂ cup/100 g/3¹/₂ oz caster sugar
¹/₄ cup/30 g/1 oz flour, sifted

WHITE CHOCOLATE ICING
100 g/3¹/₂ oz white chocolate, chopped
2 tablespoons cream (double)
sugared violets

1   Place dark chocolate and butter in a heatproof bowl set over a saucepan of simmering water and heat, stirring, until mixture is smooth. Remove bowl from pan and set aside to cool slightly.

2   Place egg yolks and sugar in a bowl and beat until thick and pale. Fold flour into

egg mixture. Add chocolate mixture to egg mixture and mix to combine.

3   Place egg whites into a clean bowl and beat until stiff peaks form. Fold egg whites into chocolate mixture.

4   Spoon mixture into greased mini cup cake tins or small paper cup cake cases and bake for 10 minutes. Remove cakes from tins and cool on wire racks.

5   To make icing, place white chocolate and cream in a heatproof bowl set over a saucepan of simmering water and heat, stirring, until mixture is smooth. Remove bowl from pan and set aside until mixture thickens slightly. Spread icing over cakes and decorate with sugared violets.

Makes 20

Sugared violets are available from cake decorators' suppliers and specialty kitchen shops.

TUILE CUPS WITH WHITE CHOCOLATE

Oven temperature
160°C, 325°F, Gas 3

ALMOND TUILE CUPS
125 g/4 oz butter, melted
4 egg whites
2 tablespoons milk
1 cup/125 g/4 oz flour
²/₃ cup/140 g/4¹/₂ oz caster sugar
60 g/2 oz flaked almonds

WHITE CHOCOLATE FILLING
250 g/8 oz white chocolate, broken into pieces
60 g/2 oz butter, chopped
¹/₄ cup/60 mL/2 fl oz cream (double)

1   To make tuiles, place butter, egg whites, milk, flour and sugar in a bowl and beat until smooth.

2   Place 2 teaspoons of mixture on a lightly greased baking tray and spread out

to make a 10 cm/4 in round. Repeat with remaining mixture leaving 10 cm/4 in between each tuile. Sprinkle with almonds and bake for 3-5 minutes or until edges of tuiles are golden. Using a spatula, carefully remove tuiles from trays and place over a small upturned strainer. Press gently to shape, then allow to cool and harden before removing from strainer.

3   To make filling, place chocolate, butter and cream in a heatproof bowl set over a saucepan of simmering water and heat, stirring, until mixture is smooth. Remove bowl from pan and set aside until mixture thickens slightly. Beat mixture until light and thick. Spoon mixture into a piping bag and pipe into tuile cups.

Makes 28

Bake only two or three tuiles at a time and work quickly, as each cup must be shaped before the biscuit cools.

Tuile Cups with White Chocolate

MARBLED SHELLS

200 g/6¹/₂ oz dark chocolate, melted
200 g/6¹/₂ oz white chocolate, melted

CREAMY CHOCOLATE FILLING
200 g/6¹/₂ oz milk chocolate
¹/₂ cup/125 mL/4 fl oz cream (double)
2 tablespoons coffee-flavoured or
hazelnut-flavoured liqueur

1   To make filling, place milk chocolate, cream and liqueur in a heatproof bowl set over a saucepan of simmering water and heat, stirring, until mixture is smooth. Remove bowl from pan and set aside until mixture cools and thickens.

3   Place a small spoonful of filling in each chocolate shell. Spoon equal quantities of the remaining dark and white chocolate over filling to fill mould. Using a skewer, carefully swirl chocolate to give marbled effect. Tap mould gently on work surface. Freeze for 3 minutes or until chocolate sets. Tap moulds gently to remove chocolates.

2   Place a teaspoon of dark chocolate and a teaspoon of white chocolate in a shell-shaped chocolate mould. Swirl with a skewer to marble chocolate and using a small brush, brush chocolate evenly over mould. Tap mould gently on work surface to remove any air bubbles. Repeat with remaining chocolate to make 30 moulds. Freeze for 2 minutes or until chocolate sets.

Makes 30

Do not overmix the white and dark chocolates or the marbled effect will diminish. Make sure the first coating sets completely before adding the filling so that the first coating does not crack.

CHOCOLATE NOUGAT HEARTS

375 g/12 oz milk chocolate, broken
into pieces
45 g/1¹/₂ oz butter, chopped
¹/₂ cup/125 mL/4 fl oz cream (double)
200 g/6¹/₂ oz nougat, chopped
100 g/3¹/₂ oz almonds, toasted, chopped

1   Place chocolate, butter and cream in a heatproof bowl set over a saucepan of simmering water and heat, stirring, until mixture is smooth.

2   Add nougat and almonds and mix well to combine. Pour mixture into a greased and lined 18 x 28 cm/7 x 11 in shallow cake tin. Refrigerate for 2 hours or until set.

3   Using a heart-shaped cutter, cut out hearts from set mixture.

Makes 40

Dip cutter into warm water
and dry on a clean towel
between each cut to
achieve evenly straight
edges.

Plate Waterford Wedgwood

48

CHOCOLATE PANFORTE

Left: Chocolate Nougat Hearts
Above: Chocolate Panforte

1 cup/250 mL/8 fl oz liquid honey
1 cup/250 g/8 oz sugar
250 g/8 oz almonds, toasted, chopped
250 g/8 oz hazelnuts, toasted, chopped
125 g/4 oz glacé apricots, chopped
125 g/4 oz glacé peaches, chopped
100 g/3$^1/_2$ oz candied mixed peel
1$^1/_2$ cups/185 g/6 oz flour, sifted
$^1/_3$ cup/45 g/1$^1/_2$ oz cocoa powder, sifted
2 teaspoons ground cinnamon
155 g/5 oz dark chocolate, melted
rice paper

1   Place honey and sugar in a small saucepan and heat, stirring constantly, over a low heat until sugar dissolves. Bring to the boil, then reduce heat and simmer, stirring constantly, for 5 minutes or until mixture thickens.

2   Place almonds, hazelnuts, apricots, peaches, mixed peel, flour, cocoa powder and cinnamon in a bowl and mix to combine. Stir in honey syrup. Add chocolate and mix well to combine.

3   Line an 18 x 28 cm/7 x 11 in shallow cake tin with rice paper. Pour mixture into tin and bake for 20 minutes. Turn onto a wire rack to cool, then cut into small pieces.

Makes 32

Oven temperature
200°C, 400°F, Gas 6

PISTACHIO TRUFFLES

315 g/10 oz dark chocolate, broken
into pieces
45 g/1^1/$_2$ oz butter, chopped
^{1}/$_2$ cup/125 mL/4 fl oz cream (double)
2 tablespoons sugar
2 tablespoons Galliano liqueur
125 g/4 oz chopped pistachio nuts

To bring out the lovely green
colour of the pistachios,
blanch the shelled nuts in
boiling water for 30 seconds,
drain and vigorously rub in a
clean towel to remove their
skins.

1   Place chocolate, butter, cream and
sugar in a heatproof bowl set over a
saucepan of simmering water and heat,
stirring, until mixture is smooth. Add
liqueur and half the pistachio nuts and
mix well to combine. Chill mixture for
1 hour or until firm enough to roll into
balls.

2   Roll tablespoons of mixture into balls,
then roll in remaining pistachio nuts.
Chill until required.

Makes 40

CARAMEL WALNUT PETITS FOURS

1 cup/250 g/8 oz sugar
^{1}/$_2$ cup/90 g/3 oz brown sugar
2 cups/500 mL/16 fl oz cream (double)
1 cup/250 mL/8 fl oz light corn or
golden syrup
60 g/2 oz butter, chopped
^{1}/$_2$ teaspoon bicarbonate of soda
155 g/5 oz chopped walnuts
1 tablespoon vanilla essence

CHOCOLATE ICING
375 g/12 oz dark or milk chocolate,
melted
2 teaspoons vegetable oil

For easy removal of the
caramel from the tin, allow
the foil lining to overhang the
tin on two opposite sides to
form handles for lifting.

1   Place sugar, brown sugar, cream, corn
or golden syrup and butter in a saucepan
and heat over a low heat, stirring
constantly, until sugar dissolves. As sugar
crystals form on sides of pan, brush with a
wet pastry brush.

2   Bring syrup to the boil and stir in
bicarbonate of soda. Reduce heat and
simmer until syrup reaches the hard ball
stage or 120°C/250°F on a sugar
thermometer.

3   Stir in walnuts and vanilla essence
and pour mixture into a greased and foil-
lined 20 cm/8 in square cake tin. Set aside
at room temperature for 5 hours or until
caramel sets.

4   Remove caramel from tin and cut into
2 cm/^{3}/$_4$ in squares.

5   To make icing, combine chocolate
and oil. Half dip caramels in melted
chocolate, place on greaseproof paper
and leave to set.

Makes 40

Pistachio Truffles, Caramel Walnut Petits Fours

SOMETHING SPECIAL

CHOCOLATE GOLD

Oven temperature
160°C, 325°F, Gas 3

The bottom of a baked cake is often smoother than the top so to ensure a perfectly smooth surface for glazing, invert the cooled cake onto another springform base or a 23 cm/9 in circle of foil-covered cardboard.

CHOCOLATE CAKE
250 g/8 oz dark chocolate, broken into pieces
155 g/5 oz butter, chopped
4 eggs, separated
³/₄ cup/185 g/6 oz sugar
¹/₃ cup/45 g/1¹/₂ oz flour, sifted
gold leaf

CHOCOLATE MIRROR GLAZE
250 g/8 oz dark chocolate, broken into pieces
3 teaspoons vegetable oil

1 To make cake, place chocolate and butter in a heatproof bowl set over a saucepan of simmering water and heat, stirring, until mixture is smooth. Remove bowl from pan and set aside to cool.

2 Place egg yolks and sugar in a bowl and beat until thick and pale. Fold flour and chocolate mixture into egg yolk mixture.

Place egg whites in a clean bowl and beat until stiff peaks form. Fold egg whites into chocolate mixture.

3 Pour mixture into a greased and lined 23 cm/9 in springform tin and bake for 30 minutes or until cake is cooked when tested with a skewer. Cool cake in tin.

4 To make glaze, place chocolate in a heatproof bowl set over a saucepan of simmering water and heat, stirring, until chocolate melts and is smooth. Stir in oil and mix until combined.

5 Remove cake from tin and place on a wire rack. Pour glaze over cake and allow it to run over sides. Leave to set. Decorate with gold leaf and serve with cream.

Serves 12

HEARTS OF CHOCOLATE

Oven temperature
190°C, 375 °F, Gas 5

To make chocolate curls see page 79.

1 quantity Simple Chocolate Cake (page 27)
cocoa powder, sifted
white chocolate curls
dark chocolate curls

CREAMY CHOCOLATE FILLING
375 g/12 oz milk chocolate, broken into pieces
155 g/5 oz butter, chopped
³/₄ cup/185 mL/6 fl oz cream (double)

1 Prepare cake as described in recipe. Pour mixture into a greased and base-lined heart-shaped cake tin and bake for 40 minutes or until cake is cooked when tested with a skewer. Stand cake in tin for 5 minutes. Turn onto a wire rack to cool.

2 Trim top of cake and turn cake upside down. Scoop out centre of cake leaving a 2 cm/³/₄ in border. Do not cut right the way through the cake, but leave 2 cm/³/₄ in cake to form the base.

3 To make filling, place chocolate, butter and cream in a heatproof bowl set over a saucepan of simmering water and heat, stirring until mixture is smooth. Remove bowl from pan and set aside to cool. Beat until light and creamy. Pour filling into prepared cake and chill for 4 hours or until filling is firm. Place cake on a serving plate. Dust top with cocoa powder and decorate with chocolate curls.

Serves 10

CHOCOLATE MASCARPONE ROULADE

Oven temperature
160°C, 325°F, Gas 3

185 g/6 oz dark chocolate
$^1/_4$ cup/60 mL/2 fl oz strong black coffee
5 eggs, separated
$^1/_2$ cup/100 g/3$^1/_2$ oz caster sugar
2 tablespoons self-raising flour, sifted
frosted rose petals

MASCARPONE FILLING
375 g/12 oz mascarpone
2 tablespoons icing sugar
2 tablespoons brandy
$^1/_2$ cup/125 g/4 oz chocolate hazelnut
spread

1 Place chocolate and coffee in a heatproof bowl set over a saucepan of simmering water and heat, stirring, until mixture is smooth. Cool slightly.

2 Beat egg yolks until thick and pale. Gradually beat in caster sugar. Fold chocolate mixture and flour into egg yolks.

3 Beat egg whites until stiff peaks form. Fold into chocolate mixture. Pour mixture into a greased and lined 26 x 32 cm/10$^1/_2$ x 12$^3/_4$ in Swiss roll tin and bake for 20 minutes or until firm. Cool in tin.

4 To make filling, beat mascarpone, icing sugar and brandy in a bowl.

5 Turn roulade onto a clean teatowel sprinkled with caster sugar. Spread with chocolate hazelnut spread and half the filling and roll up. Spread with remaining filling and decorate with frosted rose petals.

Serves 8-10

To make frosted rose petals, lightly whisk egg white in a shallow bowl and dip in fresh, dry petals to lightly cover. Dip petals into caster sugar, shake off excess and stand on greaseproof paper to harden.

*Previous pages: Hearts of Chocolate,
Chocolate Gold
Right: Chocolate Mascarpone Roulade*

Plate Waterford Wedgwood

Triple Mousse Cake

1 x 23 cm/9 in sponge cake
chocolate curls

CHOCOLATE MOUSSE
185 g/6 oz dark chocolate, melted
2 tablespoons brandy
1 egg yolk
2 egg whites
1 tablespoon sugar
$^1/_3$ cup/90 mL/3 fl oz cream (double),
whipped

MOCHA MOUSSE
185 g/6 oz milk chocolate
2 tablespoons strong black coffee
1 egg yolk
2 egg whites
1 tablespoon sugar
$^1/_3$ cup/90 mL/3 fl oz cream (double),
whipped

WHITE CHOCOLATE MOUSSE
185 g/6 oz white chocolate
2 tablespoons water
1 cup/250 mL/8 fl oz cream (double),
whipped

1   Using a serrated edged knife, cut sponge horizontally into three even layers and place one layer in base of a lined 23 cm/9 in springform tin.

2   To make Chocolate Mousse, place dark chocolate, brandy and egg yolk in a bowl and mix until smooth. Place egg whites in a clean bowl and beat until soft peaks form. Gradually beat in sugar and continue beating until stiff peaks form. Fold chocolate mixture and cream into egg whites. Pour mousse over sponge and chill for 1 hour or until mousse is firm. Top with a second layer of sponge.

3   To make Mocha Mousse, place milk chocolate, coffee and egg yolk in a bowl and mix until smooth. Place egg whites in a clean bowl and beat until soft peaks form. Gradually beat in sugar and continue beating until stiff peaks form. Fold chocolate mixture and cream into egg whites. Pour mousse over sponge and chill for 1 hour or until firm. Top with remaining sponge layer.

4   To make White Chocolate Mousse, place white chocolate and water in a heatproof bowl set over a saucepan of simmering water and heat, stirring, until mixture is smooth. Remove bowl from pan and set aside to cool slightly. Fold chocolate mixture into cream. Pour mousse over sponge. Chill for 3 hours or until firm. Just prior to serving decorate top of cake with chocolate curls.

Serves 12

Serve this elegant chocoholic's delight with a sweetened purée of fresh sieved raspberries or strawberries.

Plate Waterford Wedgwood

Triple Mousse Cake

BLACK AND WHITE TART

Oven temperature
180°C, 350°F, Gas 4

This dessert is best served the day it is made as the macaroon shell may absorb too much moisture on standing and lose its crispness.

2 egg whites
¹/₂ cup/100 g/3¹/₂ oz caster sugar
220 g/7 oz desiccated coconut
¹/₄ cup/30 g/1 oz flour, sifted

CHOCOLATE SOUR CREAM FILLING
2 egg yolks
³/₄ cup/185 mL/6 fl oz cream (double)
185 g/6 oz dark chocolate
2 tablespoons cognac or brandy
185 g/6 oz white chocolate
²/₃ cup/155 g/5 oz sour cream

RASPBERRY COULIS
250 g/8 oz raspberries
1 tablespoon icing sugar

1 Place egg whites in a bowl and beat until soft peaks form. Gradually beat in caster sugar. Fold in coconut and flour. Press mixture over base and up sides of a greased and lined 23 cm/9 in round flan tin with a removable base. Bake for 20-25 minutes or until golden. Stand in tin for 5 minutes then remove and place on a wire rack to cool.

2 To make filling, place egg yolks and cream in a heatproof bowl set over a saucepan of simmering water and beat until thick and pale. Stir in dark chocolate and cognac or brandy and continue stirring until chocolate melts. Remove bowl from pan and set aside to cool.

3 Place white chocolate and sour cream in a heatproof bowl set over a saucepan of simmering water and heat, stirring, until mixture is smooth. Remove bowl from pan and set aside to cool.

4 Place alternating spoonfuls of dark and white mixtures in macaroon shell and using a skewer swirl mixtures to give a marbled effect. Chill for 2 hours or until filling is firm.

5 To make coulis, place raspberries in a food processor or blender and process to make a purée. Press purée through a sieve to remove seeds, then stir in icing sugar. Serve with tart.

Serves 8

Black and White Tart

PINK AND WHITE MOUSSE

500 g/1 lb mixed berries of your choice
1 cup/250 g/8 oz sugar
1 tablespoon orange-flavoured liqueur
$^1/_4$ cup/60 mL/2 fl oz water
6 egg yolks
200 g/6$^1/_2$ oz white chocolate, melted
2 teaspoons vanilla essence
1$^2/_3$ cup/410 mL/13 fl oz cream
(double), whipped
white chocolate curls

1   Place berries in a food processor or blender and process to make a purée. Press purée through a sieve into a saucepan. Stir in $^1/_3$ cup/90 g/3 oz sugar and liqueur and bring to simmering over a low heat. Simmer, stirring occasionally, until mixture reduces to 1 cup/250 mL/ 8 fl oz. Remove pan from heat and set aside.

2   Place water, egg yolks and remaining sugar in a heatproof bowl set over a saucepan of simmering water and beat for 8 minutes or until mixture is light and creamy. Remove bowl from pan. Add chocolate and vanilla essence and beat until mixture cools. Fold whipped cream into chocolate mixture. Divide mixture into two portions.

3   Stir berry purée into one portion of mixture and leave one portion plain. Drop alternate spoonfuls of berry and plain mixtures into serving glasses. Using a skewer swirl mixtures to give a ripple effect. Refrigerate until firm. Just prior to serving decorate with chocolate curls.

Serves 8

Garnish with additional fresh berries or red and white currants when available.

Pink and White Mousse

CHECKERBOARD CAKE

Oven temperature
180°C, 350°F, Gas 4

2$\frac{1}{2}$ cups/315 g/10 oz flour
1 teaspoon baking powder
$\frac{3}{4}$ teaspoon bicarbonate of soda
2 cups/440 g/14 oz caster sugar
250 g/8 oz butter, softened
1$\frac{1}{2}$ cups/375 mL/12 fl oz buttermilk
or milk
60 g/2 oz white chocolate, melted
4 teaspoons vegetable oil
60 g/2 oz dark chocolate, melted
white chocolate curls

CHOCOLATE FILLING
375 g/12 oz milk chocolate, broken
into pieces
280 g/9 oz butter, chopped
1$\frac{1}{2}$ tablespoons light corn or
golden syrup

1   Sift together flour, baking powder and bicarbonate of soda in a bowl. Add sugar, butter and milk and beat until smooth. Divide mixture into two equal portions.

2   Combine white chocolate and 2 teaspoons oil and fold into one portion of mixture. Pour into a greased and lined 18 cm/7 in square cake tin.

3   Combine dark chocolate and remaining oil and fold into remaining portion of mixture. Pour into a second greased and lined 18 cm/7 in square cake tin.

4   Bake cakes for 30 minutes or until cooked when tested with a skewer. Stand cakes in tins for 5 minutes before turning onto wire racks to cool.

5   To make filling, place milk chocolate, butter and corn or golden syrup in a heatproof bowl set over a saucepan of simmering water and heat, stirring, until mixture is smooth. Remove bowl from pan and chill for 30 minutes or until filling thickens and is easy to spread.

6   To assemble cake, cut each cake into six even strips. Place a strip of white cake on a rack, spread one side with a little filling and press a strip of chocolate cake against it. Repeat with another strip of white cake and another strip of chocolate cake to make a base of alternating colours. Spread top with filling. Then use another four strips of cake to make a second layer so that colours alternate with those on the base. Spread top with filling then use remaining strips of cake to make another layer. Spread remaining filling over top and sides of cake and decorate with chocolate curls.

This pretty cake is well worth the effort and not difficult to assemble. Take your time when cutting the layers to achieve uniform pieces with straight, even edges.

Serves 12

Plate and glasses Villeroy & Boch

Checkerboard Cake

A HINT OF CHOCOLATE

CHOCOLATE PEAR TART

Oven temperature
190°C, 375°F, Gas 5

1 cup/125 g/4 oz flour
75 g/2¹/₂ oz butter
¹/₄ cup/60 g/2 oz caster sugar
2-3 tablespoons iced water
100 g/3¹/₂ oz dark chocolate, broken
into pieces
1 cup/250 mL/8 fl oz thick pure cream
1 teaspoon ground cinnamon
1 teaspoon vanilla essence
2 x 440 g/14 oz canned pear halves,
drained
¹/₂ cup/90 g/3 oz brown sugar

1   Place flour, butter and caster sugar in a food processor and process until mixture resembles fine breadcrumbs. With machine running, slowly add enough water to form a soft dough. Knead briefly. Wrap in plastic food wrap and chill for 30 minutes. Roll out pastry on a lightly floured surface to fit a 23 cm/9 in flan tin with a removable base. Line pastry shell with nonstick baking paper and fill with uncooked rice. Bake for 10 minutes. Remove rice and paper and bake for 10 minutes longer or until pastry is golden.

2   Place chocolate in a heatproof bowl set over a saucepan of simmering water and heat, stirring, until smooth. Pour chocolate over pastry base and set aside to cool.

3   Place cream, cinnamon and vanilla essence in a bowl and mix to combine. Pour cream mixture into pastry shell. Arrange pears attractively over cream and sprinkle with brown sugar. Cook tart under a preheated hot grill for 5 minutes or until golden. Serve cut into wedges.

Serves 8

Canned peach halves or slices or pitted dark sweet cherries may be used instead of the pears, if preferred.

COCONUT CAKE WITH FUDGE SAUCE

Oven temperature
160°C, 325°F, Gas 3

125 g/4 oz butter, softened
1 cup/250 g/8 oz sugar
1 teaspoon vanilla essence
4 eggs, lightly beaten
185 g/6 oz desiccated coconut
1 cup/125 g/4 oz self-raising flour, sifted
¹/₃ cup/90 g/3 oz sour cream

FUDGE SAUCE
60 g/2 oz milk chocolate, broken
into pieces
30 g/1 oz butter, chopped
2 tablespoons corn or golden syrup
1 cup/250 g/8 oz sugar
³/₄ cup/185 mL/6 fl oz cream (double)

1   Place butter, sugar and vanilla essence in a bowl and beat until light and fluffy. Gradually beat in eggs. Stir coconut, flour and sour cream into butter mixture and mix until combined.

2   Pour mixture into a greased and lined 20 cm/8 in round cake tin and bake for 35 minutes. Stand in tin while making sauce.

3   To make sauce, place chocolate, butter and corn or golden syrup in a saucepan and heat over a low heat, stirring, until mixture is smooth. Add sugar and cream and cook, stirring, until sugar dissolves. Bring to the boil, then reduce heat and simmer for 8 minutes or until sauce thickens. Serve with warm cake.

Serves 8

A scoop of vanilla ice cream goes well with this. Leftover fudge sauce can be stored in a covered container in the refrigerator. Reheat sauce in a heatproof bowl set over hot water and stir until smooth.

Previous pages: Chocolate Pear Tart, Coconut Cake with Fudge Sauce
Fabric Wardlaw
Right: Cassata Layers

CASSATA LAYERS

1 x 20 cm/8 in sponge cake
¼ cup/60 mL/2 fl oz almond-flavoured liqueur
chocolate curls

CASSATA FILLING
1 litre/1¾ pt vanilla ice cream, softened
1 cup/250 mL/8 fl oz cream (double)
125 g/4 oz glacé apricots, chopped
125 g/4 oz glacé pineapple, chopped
60 g/2 oz glacé cherries, chopped
60 g/2 oz raisins, halved
125 g/4 oz dark chocolate, grated
125 g/4 oz pistachio nuts, chopped

1   To make filling place ice cream, cream, apricots, pineapple, cherries, raisins, chocolate and pistachio nuts in a bowl and mix to combine.

2   Split sponge horizontally into three even layers. Place one layer of sponge in the base of a lined 20 cm/8 in springform tin and sprinkle with 1 tablespoon of liqueur. Top with one-third of the filling. Repeat layers to use all ingredients ending with a layer of filling. Freeze for 5 hours or until firm. Remove from freezer 1 hour before serving and place in refrigerator.

3   Just prior to serving, decorate with chocolate curls.

Serves 10

Use the best quality ice cream you can afford. To retain maximum volume and creamy texture, keep the cassata filling mixture well chilled until the cassata is finally assembled.

Plate Villeroy & Boch *Fabric Wardlaw*

CITRUS PUDDING WITH CHOC SAUCE

90 g/3 oz butter, softened
$^1/_3$ cup/75 g/2$^1/_2$ oz caster sugar
2 eggs, lightly beaten
1 cup/125 g/4 oz self-raising flour, sifted
$^1/_4$ cup/60 mL/2 fl oz buttermilk or milk
2 tablespoons lemon curd
2 tablespoons finely grated orange rind

RICH CHOCOLATE SAUCE
60 g/2 oz butter
200 g/6$^1/_2$ oz dark chocolate, broken
into pieces
1 cup/250 mL/8 fl oz cream (double)
2 tablespoons orange-flavoured liqueur

1   Place butter and sugar in a bowl and beat until light and fluffy. Gradually beat in eggs. Add flour, milk, lemon curd and orange rind and mix well to combine.

2   Spoon mixture into a greased 4 cup/ 1 litre/1$^3/_4$ pt capacity pudding basin and cover with aluminium foil and secure with pudding basin lid. Place basin on a wire rack in a large saucepan with enough boiling water to come halfway up the side of the basin. Cover and boil for 1$^1/_4$ hours or until pudding is cooked when tested with a skewer, replacing water if necessary as pudding cooks.

3   To make sauce, place butter, chocolate, cream and liqueur in a heatproof bowl set over a saucepan of simmering water and heat, stirring, until mixture is smooth. Serve with pudding.

Slice pudding into wedges and pour sauce over pudding. Serve with a scoop of ice cream.

Serves 6

CARAMEL ORANGE CHEESECAKE

3 oranges
$^1/_2$ cup/125 mL/4 fl oz rum
$^1/_2$ cup/90 g/3 oz brown sugar

CHOCOLATE BASE
250 g/8 oz plain chocolate biscuits,
crushed
125 g/4 oz butter, melted
2 tablespoons caster sugar

ORANGE FILLING
250 g/8 oz cream cheese
125 g/4 oz ricotta cheese
$^1/_2$ cup/125 g/4 oz sugar
1 cup/250 mL/8 fl oz cream (double)
$^2/_3$ cup/155 g/5 oz sour cream
3 eggs, lightly beaten
2 tablespoons flour
2 tablespoons finely grated orange rind
1 tablespoon orange flower water or
orange juice

CARAMEL SAUCE
$^1/_2$ cup/125 g/4 oz sugar
$^1/_4$ cup/60 mL/2 fl oz water

1 Remove zest from oranges and set
aside. Remove white pith from oranges.
Cut oranges crosswise into 1 cm/$^1/_2$ in
thick slices. Place rum and brown sugar in
a bowl and mix to combine. Add orange
slices and set aside to stand for 1 hour.

2 To make base, combine biscuit
crumbs, butter and caster sugar in a bowl.
Press mixture over base and up sides of a
greased and lined 20 cm/8 in springform
tin.

3 To make filling, place cream cheese,
ricotta cheese, sugar, cream, sour cream,
eggs, flour, orange rind and orange flower
water or orange juice into a food processor
and process until smooth.

4 Pour filling into tin and bake for
50 minutes or until firm. Cool in tin.

5 To make sauce, place sugar and water
in a saucepan and heat over a low heat,
stirring, until sugar dissolves. Bring to the
boil, then reduce heat and simmer until
syrup is golden. Drain orange slices and
arrange attractively on top of cheesecake.
Pour sauce over cheesecake and serve.

Serves 8-10

Oven temperature
160°C, 325°F, Gas 3

Decorate this dessert with its
sliced oranges and caramel
sauce just prior to serving.

Left: Citrus Pudding with Choc Sauce
Right: Caramel Orange Cheesecake

Plate Waterford Wedgwood

FROZEN MAPLE NUT PARFAIT

6 egg yolks
1 cup/220 g/7 oz caster sugar
1/2 cup/125 mL/4 fl oz water
1/2 cup/125 mL/4 fl oz maple syrup
600 mL/1 pt cream (double)
100 g/3 1/2 oz macadamia nuts, finely
chopped
100 g/3 1/2 oz white chocolate, chopped
extra maple syrup

This light and luscious frozen Italian meringue is the perfect partner for a garnish of fresh fruit and perhaps some almond-flavoured biscotti.

1   Place egg yolks in a bowl and beat until thick and pale. Place sugar and water in a saucepan and heat over a low heat, stirring, until sugar dissolves. Bring mixture to the boil and boil until mixture thickens and reaches soft ball stage or 118°C/244°F on a sugar thermometer.

2   Gradually beat sugar syrup and maple syrup into egg yolks and continue beating until mixture cools. Place cream in a bowl and beat until soft peaks form. Fold cream, macadamia nuts and chocolate into egg mixture.

3   Pour mixture into an aluminium foil-lined 15 x 25 cm/6 x 10 in loaf tin and freeze for 5 hours or until firm.

4   Turn parfait onto a serving plate, remove foil, cut into slices and drizzle with maple syrup.

Serves 8

BANANA MOUSSE

1 tablespoon gelatine
1/4 cup/60 mL/2 fl oz boiling water
500 g/1 lb ripe bananas
1/4 cup/60 g/2 oz sugar
1 tablespoon lemon juice
220 mL/7 fl oz cream (double)
100 mL/3 1/2 fl oz coconut milk
100 g/3 1/2 oz dark chocolate, melted

When available, dried banana chips make an attractive garnish with fresh mint leaves.

1   Place gelatine and boiling water in a bowl and stir until gelatine dissolves. Set aside to cool.

2   Place bananas, sugar and lemon juice in a food processor and process until smooth. Stir gelatine mixture into banana mixture.

3   Place cream and coconut milk in a bowl and beat until soft peaks form. Fold cream mixture into banana mixture.

4   Spoon mousse into six serving glasses. Divide melted chocolate between glasses and swirl with a skewer. Refrigerate for 2 hours or until set.

Serves 6

Banana Mousse, Frozen Maple Nut Parfait

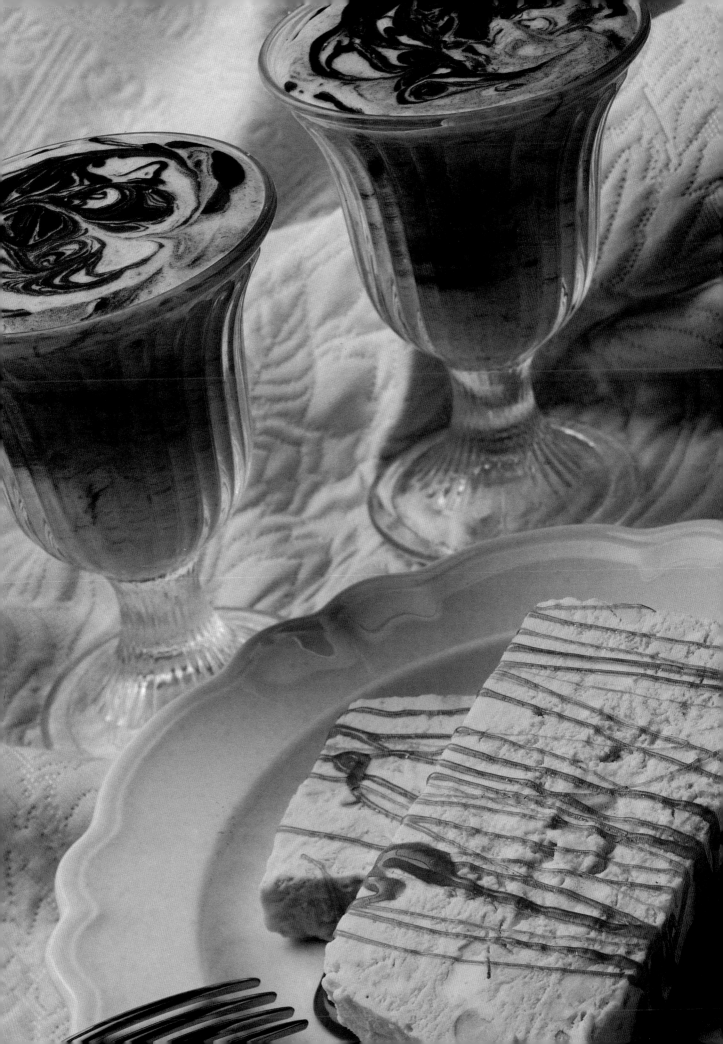

FESTIVE
CHOCOLATE

YULE LOG

Oven temperature
180°C, 350°F, Gas 4

5 eggs, separated
$^1/_4$ cup/60 g/2 oz caster sugar
100 g/3$^1/_2$ oz dark chocolate, melted and
cooled
2 tablespoons self-raising flour, sifted
2 tablespoons cocoa powder, sifted
chocolate shavings

WHITE CHOCOLATE FILLING
60 g/2 oz white chocolate
$^2/_3$ cup/170 mL/5$^1/_2$ fl oz cream (double)

CHOCOLATE ICING
200 g/6$^1/_2$ oz dark chocolate, melted
60 g/2 oz butter, melted

1   Place egg yolks and sugar in a bowl and
beat until thick and pale. Stir in
chocolate, flour and cocoa powder.

2   Place egg whites in a clean bowl and
beat until stiff peaks form. Fold egg whites
into chocolate mixture.

3   Pour mixture into a greased and lined
26 x 32 cm/10$^1/_2$ x 12$^3/_4$ in Swiss roll tin
and bake for 15 minutes or until firm.
Turn cake onto a teatowel sprinkled with
caster sugar and roll up from short end.
Set aside to cool.

4   To make filling, place white chocolate
in a heatproof bowl set over a saucepan
of simmering water and heat, stirring,
until smooth. Add cream and stir
until combined. Cover and chill until
thickened and of a spreadable consistency.

5   Unroll cake and spread with filling
leaving a 1 cm/$^1/_2$ in border. Re-roll cake.

6   To make icing, combine chocolate
and butter and mix until combined.
Spread icing over roll then, using a fork,
roughly texture the icing. Decorate with
chocolate shavings.

Serves 8

Keep this dessert refrigerated
until served. Dust log with
icing sugar to create 'snow'
just before serving.

FRUIT AND NUT WREATH

1$^1/_2$ cups/375 g/12 oz sugar
$^3/_4$ cup/185 mL/6 fl oz water
$^3/_4$ cup/185 mL/6 fl oz cream (double)
315 g/10 oz roasted unsalted mixed nuts
125 g/4 oz dried apricots
90 g/3 oz raisins
125 g/4 oz glacé pineapple, chopped
125 g/4 oz glacé cherries
125 g/4 oz dark chocolate, melted

1   Place sugar and water in a saucepan
and heat over a low heat, stirring, until
sugar dissolves. Bring to the boil, then
reduce heat and simmer for 6 minutes or
until syrup is golden.

2   Remove pan from heat and carefully
stir in cream. Return pan to heat and
cook, stirring, until mixture is smooth.

3   Place nuts, apricots, raisins, pineapple
and cherries in a heatproof bowl. Pour
caramel over fruit mixture and mix well
to combine. Pour mixture into a greased
and lined 20 cm/8 in ring tin. Allow to
set.

4   Remove wreath from tin and drizzle
with melted chocolate.

Serves 8

This delicious treat makes a
beautiful holiday gift when
presented in a see-through
box wrapped with green or
red satin ribbon.

*Previous pages: Fruit and Nut
Wreath, Yule Log*
Patterned plate Villeroy & Boch
*Right: Ice Cream Christmas
Pudding*

ICE CREAM CHRISTMAS PUDDING

1 litre/1³/₄ pt chocolate ice cream,
softened
125 g/4 oz glacé **apricots**, chopped
125 g/4 oz glacé **cherries**, chopped
125 g/4 oz glacé **pears**, chopped
90 g/3 oz **sultanas**
75 g/2¹/₂ oz **raisins**, chopped
2 tablespoons **rum**

1   Place ice cream, apricots, cherries,
pears, sultanas, raisins and rum in a bowl
and mix to combine. Pour into an oiled
and lined 6 cup/1.5 litre/2¹/₂ pt capacity
pudding basin.

2   Freeze for 3 hours or until firm.

Serves 8

To help unmould the
pudding, briefly hold a warm
damp teatowel around the
outside of the mould. To
serve, slice pudding and
serve with rum custard.

Plate Waterford Wedgwood Fabric Redelman & Son

CHRISTMAS STOCKING BISCUITS

Oven temperature
180°C, 350°F, Gas 4

125 g/4 oz butter
³/₄ cup/125 g/4 oz icing sugar
1 egg
1¹/₄ cups/155 g/5 oz flour
1¹/₄ cups/155 g/5 oz self-raising flour
90 g/3 oz dark chocolate, melted
60 g/2 oz milk chocolate, melted

1 Place butter, icing sugar, egg, flour and self-raising flour in a food processor and process until a soft dough forms. Knead dough briefly, wrap in plastic food wrap and chill for 30 minutes.

2 Roll out dough on nonstick baking paper to 5 mm/¹/₄ in thick.

3 Using a template of a Christmas stocking or a Christmas stocking cookie cutter, cut stocking shapes and place on a greased baking tray. Bake for 10 minutes or until biscuits are golden. Transfer to a wire rack to cool.

3 Dip tops of stockings in dark chocolate to make a 1 cm/¹/₂ in border. Allow to set.

4 Dip biscuits into milk chocolate half way up dark chocolate. Allow to set.

Use any leftover melted chocolate to pipe designs onto the stockings, if desired.

Makes 24

Plate, cup and saucer/Waterford Wedgwood

TRUFFLE EASTER EGGS

Left: Christmas Stocking Biscuits
Above: Truffle Easter Eggs

125 g/4 oz dark chocolate, melted

TRUFFLE FILLING
$^1/_2$ cup/125 mL/4 fl oz cream (double)
250 g/8 oz milk chocolate
1 tablespoon golden syrup

1 Place a spoonful of dark chocolate in a small easter egg mould and use a small paint brush to evenly coat. Freeze for 2 minutes or until chocolate sets. Repeat with remaining chocolate to make 32 shells.

2 To make filling, place cream in a saucepan and bring to the boil. Remove pan from heat, add milk chocolate and stir until smooth. Stir in golden syrup and chill for 20 minutes or until mixture is thick enough to pipe.

3 Spoon filling into a piping bag fitted with a star-shaped nozzle and pipe filling into chocolate shells.

Makes 32

TECHNIQUES

The source of chocolate, the cacao tree,
was one of the greatest discoveries made on the American
continent. Chocolate's scientific name is Theobroma cacao –
theobroma *means 'food of the gods'.*

STORING CHOCOLATE

Chocolate should be stored in a dry, airy place at a temperature of about 16°C/60°F. If stored in unsuitable conditions, the cocoa butter in chocolate may rise to the surface, leaving a white film. A similar discoloration occurs when water condenses on the surface. This often happens to refrigerated chocolates that are too loosely wrapped. Chocolate affected in this way is still suitable for melting, however it is unsuitable for grating.

MELTING CHOCOLATE

Chocolate melts more rapidly if broken into small pieces. The melting process should occur slowly, as chocolate scorches if overheated. To melt chocolate, place the chocolate in the top of a double saucepan or in a bowl set over a saucepan of simmering water and heat, stirring, until chocolate melts and is smooth. Alternatively, chocolate can be melted in the microwave. To melt 375 g/12 oz chocolate, break it into small pieces and place in a microwavable glass or ceramic bowl or jug and cook on HIGH (100%) for $1^1/_2$-2 minutes. Stir. If the chocolate is not completely melted cook for 30-45 seconds longer. When melting chocolate in the microwave you should be aware that it holds its shape and it is important to stir it frequently so that it does not burn.

❦ The container in which the chocolate is being melted should be kept uncovered and completely dry. Covering could cause condensation and just one drop of water will ruin the chocolate.

❦ Chocolate 'seizes' if it is overheated, or if it comes into contact with water or steam. Seizing results in the chocolate tightening and becoming a thick mass that will not melt. To rescue seized chocolate, stir in a little cream or vegetable oil, until the chocolate becomes smooth again.

Chocolate Leaves

Choose non-poisonous, fresh, stiff leaves with raised veins. Retain as much stem as possible. Wash leaves, then dry well on absorbent kitchen paper. Brush the underside of the leaves with melted chocolate and allow to set at room temperature. When set, carefully peel away leaf. Use one leaf to decorate an individual dessert, or a make a bunch and use to decorate a large dessert or cake.

Piped Chocolate Decorations

These are quick and easy to make. Trace a simple design onto a sheet of paper. Tape a sheet of baking or greaseproof paper to your work surface and slide the drawings under the paper. Place melted chocolate into a paper or material piping bag and, following the tracings, pipe thin lines. Allow to set at room temperature and then carefully remove, using a metal spatula. If you are not going to use these decorations immediately, store them in an airtight container in a cool place.

Chocolate Cases

To make chocolate cases, quarter fill the mould with melted chocolate and tap to remove any air bubbles. Brush chocolate evenly up sides of mould to make a shell, then freeze for 2 minutes or until set. Larger chocolate cases to hold desserts can also be made in this way using foil-lined individual metal flan tins, brioche or muffin tins as moulds. When set, remove from tins and fill with dessert filling such as mousse or a flavoured cream.

CHOCOLATE CARAQUES

These are made by spreading a layer of melted chocolate over a marble, granite or ceramic work surface. Allow the chocolate to set at room temperature. Then, holding a metal pastry scraper or a large knife at a 45° angle slowly push it along the work surface away from you to form the chocolate into cylinders. If chocolate shavings form, then it is too cold and it is best to start again.

CHOCOLATE CURLS OR SHAVINGS

Chocolate curls are made from chocolate that is at room temperature. To make shavings, chill the chocolate first. Using a vegetable peeler, shave the sides of the chocolate. Whether curls or shavings form depends on the temperature of the chocolate.

MAKING A PAPER PIPING BAG

1   Cut a 25 cm/10 in square of greaseproof paper.

2   Cut square in half digonally to form two triangles.

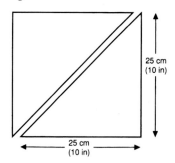

3   To make piping bag, place paper triangles on top of each other and mark the three corners A, B and C.

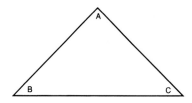

4   Fold corner B around and inside corner A.

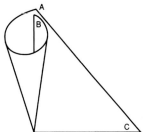

5   Bring corner C around the outside of the bag until it fits exactly behind corner A. At this stage all three corners should be together and point closed.

6   Fold corner A over two or three times to hold the bag together.

7   Snip the point off the bag and drop in icing nozzle. The piping bag can also be used without a nozzle for writing and outlines, in which case only the very tip of the point should be snipped off the bag.

To fill the piping bag: Spoon chocolate or icing into the bag to half fill. Fold the top over about 1 cm/^{1}/$_2$ in then fold over again. Fold the tips towards the centre and press with your thumb on the join to force the chocolate or icing out.

Holding the piping bag: To hold the piping bag correctly, grip the bag near the top with the folded or twisted end held between the thumb and fingers. Guide the bag with your free hand. Right-handed people should decorate from left to right, while left-handers will decorate from right to left, the exception being when piping writing.

The appearance of your piping will be directly affected by how you squeeze and relax your grip on the piping bag, that is, the pressure that you apply and the steadiness of that pressure. The pressure should be so consistent that you can move the bag in a free and easy glide with just the right amount of chocolate or icing flowing from the nozzle. A little practice will soon have you feeling confident.

INDEX

ACKNOWLEDGMENTS

The publisher thanks the following companies who generously supplied props for this book.

Appley Hoare Antiques
55 Queen St, Woollahra,
Sydney
Ph: (02) 362 3045

Limoges Australia
Available from David
Jones and Georges
(Melbourne)
Ph: (02) 328 6876

Orrefors Kosta Boda
Available from Orrefors
Kosta Boda Corporate
Stores, David Jones and
selected stores

Redelman & Son Pty Ltd
37 Ocean St, Woollahra,
Sydney
Ph: (02) 328 6413

Villeroy & Boch
Available from major
department stores and
gift suppliers
Ph: (02) 975 3099
enquiries

Wardlaw Pty Ltd
Furnishings Wholesalers
Ph: (02) 660 6266
enquires

Waterford Wedgwood
Australia Limited
Available from major
department stores and
leading speciality stores
Ph: (02) 899 2877